Cutting-Edge Research in Developing the Library of the Future

Creating the 21st-Century Academic Library

About the Series

Creating the 21st-Century Academic Library provides both conceptual information and practical guidance on the full spectrum of innovative changes now underway in academic libraries. Each volume in the series is carefully crafted to be a hallmark of professional practice and thus:

- Focuses on one narrowly defined aspect of academic librarianship.
- Features an introductory chapter, surveying the content to follow and highlighting lessons to be learned.
- Shares the experiences of librarians who have recently overseen significant changes in their library to better position it to provide 21st-century services to students, faculty, and researchers.

About the Series Editor

Bradford Lee Eden is one of librarianship's most experienced and knowledgeable editors. Dr. Eden is dean of library services at Valparaiso University. Previous positions include associate university librarian for technical services and scholarly communication at the University of California, Santa Barbara; head of web and digitization services and head of bibliographic and metadata services for the University of Nevada, Las Vegas Libraries. He is editor of *OCLC Systems & Services: International Digital Library Perspectives* and *The Bottom Line: Managing Library Finances*, and he is on the editorial boards of *Library Hi Tech* and the *Journal of Film Music*. He has recently been named associate editor/editor-designate of *Library Leadership & Management*, the journal of the Library Leadership & Management Association (LLAMA) within ALA.

Titles in the Series

Cutting-Edge Research in Developing the Library of the Future

New Paths for Building Future Services

Edited by Bradford Lee Eden

ROWMAN & LITTLEFIELD
Lanham • Boulder • New York • London

Published by Rowman & Littlefield
A wholly owned subsidiary of The Rowman & Littlefield Publishing Group, Inc.
4501 Forbes Boulevard, Suite 200, Lanham, Maryland 20706
www.rowman.com

Unit A, Whitacre Mews, 26-34 Stannary Street, London SE11 4AB

British Library Cataloguing in Publication Information Available

Library of Congress Cataloging-in-Publication Data

Cutting-edge research in developing the library of the future : New paths for building future services /
edited by Bradford Lee Eden.
pages cm. — (Creating the 21st-century academic library ; 3)
Includes bibliographical references and index.
ISBN 978-1-4422-5045-1 (hardcover : alk. paper) — ISBN 978-1-4422-5046-8 (pbk. : alk. paper) —
ISBN 978-1-4422-5047-5 (ebook)
1. Academic libraries—Administration. 2. Academic libraries—Information technology. 3. Libraries—Special collections—Electronic information resources. 4. Academic librarians—Effect of technological innovations on. I. Eden, Bradford Lee, editor.
Z675.U5.C88 2015
025.1'977—dc23
2015004924

Printed in the United States of America

Contents

Introduction

This book examines cutting-edge research in developing the library of the future. Lauren Magnuson starts by discussing how predictive analytics, a set of techniques that combines data-mining and business-intelligence metrics to predict future trends and behaviors, can be adapted for use in academic libraries. She distinguishes between similar concepts such as predictive business analytics (PBA), predictive analytics, business intelligence, data mining, and predictive models and then moves into examples of what libraries should measure, planning and deploying a predictive analytics project, and some of the methods and tools needed to do so. Magnuson then examines learning analytics, along with issues related to privacy and ethics, ending with an emphasis on how important data collection will be as a skill set for librarians and libraries in the future.

April Grey and Rachel Isaac-Menard challenge the library profession to consider new services related to the proliferation of mobile devices among patrons. They discuss the eCampus portal available at Adelphi University and how a redesign opportunity allowed the library to assist the campus in porting their information to mobile devices. The design of various icons, along with integration of the campus's Moodle infrastructure, sets up some interesting challenges and connections. The authors provide a summary of the experience, along with lessons learned and future considerations for the collaboration.

Ian Demsky and Suzanne Chapman provide concrete examples of how one large research university library dealt with a massive website overhaul. They provide background about the decentralized web content strategy first instituted at the University of Michigan libraries in 1997 and their attempts to rein in overall management and strategy of the libraries' website in a cultural environment where individual and departmental expression regarding website presence had not been challenged in a long time. The approach of using a web content strategist and an empowered team of nine web content coordinators to start the process, which then moved to a web content coordinator group, is documented along with all of the subsequent issues related to culture change and the overall learning curve that comes with it. In the end, the process is still evolving and growing, and the website continues to move forward in its new direction.

Laura Staley shows how video production can be used by the academic library for marketing, instruction, navigation, and reaching patrons in social media sites. She provides step-by-step guidelines for producing videos, including pros and cons, planning, best practices, and resources already available, equipment needs, video-production activities, editing and accessibility, and marketing.

Dawn Paschal and her team provide a literature review and recommendations on the topic of incorporating mobile information technologies in libraries, a fairly comprehensive and detailed annotated report that is highly useful for the profession.

The contribution by Shannon Regan provides an overall viewpoint of skills needed to manage electronic resources in a digital campus environment. These skills include an understanding of the collection, licensing, tracking and providing access, troubleshooting, and assessment. Amy Fry continues this discussion by focusing on organizational structure, workflows, and training for librarians and library staff in relation to e-resources, documenting her experiences at Bowling Green State University.

Finally, Cory Lampert and Silvia Southwick explore how linked open data (LOD) has transformed library workflows, staff expertise, and traditional metadata creation at the University of Nevada–Las Vegas, and how various pilot projects have assisted in overall learning and development of using LOD in the future within their library and part of the larger data community.

All of these examples of futuristic and exciting new library services and workflows provide opportunities and experiences that the rest of the library profession can model and adapt for their own particular communities and patrons. It is hoped that this volume will add to that overall knowledge and provide pathways for others to follow and create.

Chapter One

Predictive Analytics in Libraries

Lauren Magnuson

It is a capital mistake to theorize before one has data. Insensibly one begins to twist facts to suit theories, instead of theories to suit facts.
—Sherlock Holmes, *A Study in Scarlet*

Predictive analytics is an emerging set of techniques that utilizes business-intelligence metrics and data mining to predict future behaviors or trends. While the terms *business intelligence data mining,* and *predictive analytics* sometimes seem to be interchangeable, there are key distinctions between each of the concepts:

- *Business intelligence* (BI) refers to historical analysis of data gathered in an organization. Business intelligence is often used to synthesize, summarize, and report on historical data but does not usually attempt to predict future trends.
- *Data mining* (sometimes referred to as "big data") refers to the process of discovering knowledge and identifying patterns within large sets of data and is the procedural underpinning of many analytics projects (Han and Kamber, 2006).
- *Analytics* refers to the process of "data extraction using efficient, reproducible, and scalable algorithms" and often involves summarizing results from data-mining processes (Schwartz, 2011, p. 66).
- *Predictive analytics* or *predictive business analytics* (PBA) "reflects an organizational capability to improve managerial decision making across many core performance areas" (Maisel and Cokins, 2014, p. 22).
- A *predictive model* is "a mechanism that predicts a behavior of an individual. . . . It takes characteristics of the individual as input, and provides a predictive score as output" (Siegel, 2013, p. 26).

As Maisel and Cokins (2014) write, "What distinguishes predictive business analytics (PBA) is that the decision-making process is rooted in a structured, continuous, and data-driven process that enables an organization to select actions with a fair degree of understanding of how these decisions and actions were determined to have a reasonable level of confidence regarding outcomes and impacts" (p. 44). Each of these techniques, however, must be guided by a decision-making process that helps to identify problems that can shape how these techniques are deployed.

Applied to libraries, predictive analytics could more accurately predict the level of staff needed at a reference desk during certain hours and certain times of the year, the number of copies of a particular book that should be available at a particular time, or what kinds of research topics are likely to trend in the very near future—and many of these insights could be made available to decision makers in a more or less automated fashion. As libraries move toward a data-driven and user-driven service and acquisition model, predictive analytics has the potential to meet users' needs in ways only previously imagined.

Predictive analytics also has the practical potential of helping library administrators determine in which services to invest time, staff, and limited funding. As libraries are increasingly constrained by shrinking budgets and are under pressure to produce evidence of accountability, libraries need to be able to analyze data to help illustrate trends, to predict opportunities for service growth, and to justify new expenditures (Massis, 2012).

Data-mining projects can be complex, but the first step to any analytics project is to determine what insight is expected to be gained. Prior to considering which data points should be gathered, clearly identifying a problem that needs to be solved can serve to effectively guide a data analytics project through a potential ocean of data.

WHAT SHOULD WE MEASURE?

Libraries have traditionally gathered lots of statistics that aggregate how much the library is being used overall: circulation, foot and click traffic, questions asked at the desk, and other transactional data points. The power of predictive analytics is that the mechanisms for analysis can take big aggregate data and assess the small connections that can help to make very specific predictions. Predictive analytics has provided insight and improved decision making in several contexts, with impacts that can be both large scale and precise:

- One of the most famous examples of the application of predictive analytics is its use by a team of over fifty analytics experts working for President

Obama's 2012 reelection campaign (Siegel, 2013). Specifically, the campaign utilized a process called *uplift modeling* or *persuasion modeling* to determine what kinds of contact (flyers, phone calls, or door-to-door visits) were likely to be effective on particular voters—especially elusive "swing voters" who could potentially be convinced to vote for either candidate. In some cases, campaign contact of any kind may have influenced a particular voter to vote *against* the candidate, and to predict how to avoid that outcome was of particular importance to the campaign. By conducting sample contacts with voter groups, collecting data on the outcome of the contact (how likely the voter was to vote for the candidate), and studying the demographics of those voters, the strategy was able "to convince more voters to choose Obama over traditional campaign targeting" (Siegel, 2013, p. 217).

• Predictive modeling is starting to be employed to help predict factors that contribute to student success and retention in higher education. For example, several projects have developed methods to help predict college student persistence and retention (Alkhasawneh and Hobson, 2011), while other models have been developed to help identify students at risk for failing or not completing a course (du Plessis and Botha, 2012; Lauría et al., 2013; Oladokun, Adebanjo, and Charles-Owaba, 2008). Such modeling has the potential to provide instructional designers and educators with valuable insight into "a vital link between instruction, assessment, and student effort" (Baepler and Murdoch, 2010, p. 4).

"Big data" or data-mining projects tend to be discussed in reference to large-scale projects that have the potential to impact major strategic areas of an organization—and major impact can certainly be the case. But one of the key benefits of having large data points at one's fingertips is the ability to make *small connections* at the level of individual users or transactions and use those connections to identify patterns over time. It is often the case that interesting patterns emerge from data that were not anticipated when data collection began.

To help identify an area where predictive analytics could improve library services, consider user behavior in your library that seems difficult to predict or inconsistent. For example, perhaps some library events are extraordinarily successful and there isn't enough space to accommodate all attendees while other events have almost no attendance despite every effort to advertise the event. Another example might be a particular subject collection in a university library that has disproportionately low use compared to the number of students and faculty members the collection is designed to serve. By looking closely at existing usage patterns and user behavior, *use cases* (narratives describing the potential applications of a project) begin to emerge that can inform the design of a predictive model.

USE CASES AND PLANNING

The first step to beginning a predictive analytics project is to identify a problem that requires more information or data to solve than is currently available. You probably have some anecdotal observations of trends you suspect but don't have data to confirm or refute those suspicions. These observations can be used to create a use case that describes how predictive data might be used to improve processes or services (Schmarzo, 2013). Defining use cases is an integral part of planning a predictive analytics project that helps stakeholders envision the potential impact of the project and can facilitate clarifying how the project aligns with organizational values and goals (Massis, 2012).

For example, consider the following problem that many libraries encounter: circulation of print books tends to be decreasing, while use of e-books tends to be increasing. Anecdotal reports from librarians, however, indicate that students seem to have a preference for print. Librarians may have experienced recommending e-books to students at the reference desk, only for the student to reply, "I hate e-books, do you have something on the shelf that I can just check out?"

With these kinds of experiences, librarians can face a quandary concerning collection-development decisions: Do they respond to the statistical usage trends, which seem to indicate that e-book usage is going up, or do they respond to their in-person experiences, which seem to indicate a student preference for print?

In this use case, decision makers (librarians and library leadership) need to know the following:

- *Who* (in other words, what are the demographics, interests, fields of study, etc.) are e-book users? Who are print users?
- *What factors* (behaviors or experiences) predict a format preference (either print or digital)?
- When a particular format is preferred, *what variables* predict how much that book will be used? In other words, which format should be chosen of a particular title to maximize usage?

Maisel and Cokins (2014) identify two major elements of predictive business analytics (PBA): *structural elements*, which occur first and include process design, model development, and data capture; and *deployment*, which involves analyzing, reporting, and facilitating decision making in an ongoing or automated manner. For predictive analytics to have a genuine impact on organizational processes, predictive data must be accessible by decision makers and integrated into existing workflows. As Schmarzo (2013) writes, "Instead of delivering a traditional business-intelligence user interface with a multitude of charts and graphics and the promise of 'slicing and dicing,' instead we can leverage big data capabilities to tease out and deliver only those insights (and corresponding recommendations) that are of interest to the business stakeholders and material to the business" (p. 105).

In this example use case, *deployment* could involve creating a user interface that librarians can access that predicts whether a particular title, if purchased, is more likely to be used in digital format or in print format—or whether it is likely to be used at all.

The variables used to construct such a predictive model will vary by organizational needs. For example, a predictive model can weight factors relatively, such as the book's subject, length, reading level, specificity of topic, author, and publisher. Combined with business-intelligence data on the library's user behavior, such a model could be used to predict how likely the book would circulate. For libraries using demand-driven acquisition (DDA) models, such prediction could help predict the budget needed to fully fund demand-driven purchases. Armed with a predictive model that shows the frequency with which a particular title would be used, libraries could make more informed decisions about what kind of access or license should be purchased.

This is an overly simplified example designed to provide an overview of a hypothetical predictive analytics project. A process like the one described above would take a significant investment in time, staff, and resources to develop. Moreover, predictive models are not perfect and should not be used as the sole factor in decision making but rather to support decision-making processes (Greller and Drachsler, 2012); however, when dealing with complex problems that affect a library's bottom line—such as the return on investment of resource acquisition—this type of project has the potential to significantly improve collection-development and day-to-day organizational practices in a library.

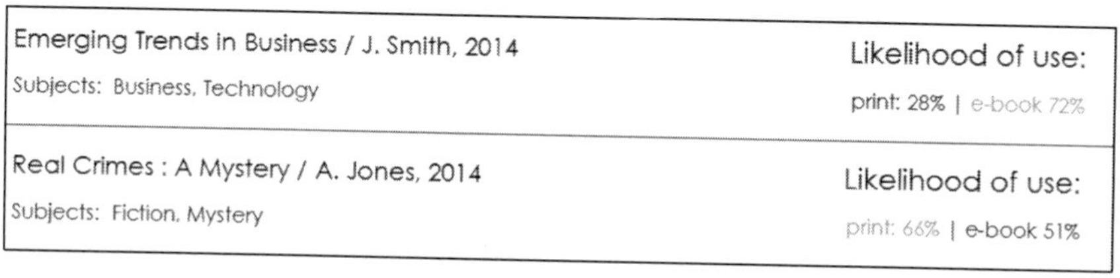

Emerging Trends in Business / J. Smith, 2014

Subjects: Business, Technology

Likelihood of use:

print: 28% | e-book 72%

Real Crimes : A Mystery / A. Jones, 2014

Subjects: Fiction, Mystery

Likelihood of use:

print: 66% | e-book 51%

Figure 1.1.   Mockup of how a predictive model can be deployed to improve day-to-day decision making. A predictive model could be used to predict which format (e-book or print) is more likely to be used.

Chapter 1

METHODS AND TOOLS

While a general understanding of statistical analysis and regression statistics is essential for working with predictive analytics, there are a few key mathematical concepts and software tools that are commonly used and discussed in predictive analytics and predictive modeling:

Mathematical Models

While this list is by no means comprehensive, some of the more common methods employed by predictive models include the following:

Regression analysis. Regression analysis is one of the most fundamental methods of developing a predictive model. As James Wu (2012) writes, "It is likely that 90% or more of real world applications of data mining end up with a relatively simple regression as the final model, typically after very careful data preparation, encoding and creation of variables" (p. 83). In regression analysis, the relationship between a dependent variable (usually an outcome, like number of e-books downloaded per month) and independent variables (such as the number of e-readers or tablets purchased in the previous month) can be analyzed. This method analyzes how the dependent variable is affected by changes with the independent variable, usually expressed as a probability distribution (Maisel and Cokins, 2014).

Neural network model. A neural network utilizes a set of connected input and output units, where each connection has an associated weight (Han and Kamber, 2006). Neural networks are considered to "learn" over time by modifying the weights to better organize data into classes. These classes can then be used to understand relationships between classes—and neural network methods work well applied to situations where data is "noisy" or you are unsure of the relationships among existing variables (Han and Kamber, 2006). When data is input into a neural network system, the network runs through the initial data sample thousands of times until an optimal solution is found and the weights that define neural network connections are no longer modified significantly with additional passes over the sample (Tufféry, 2011). The model generated by learning can then be used in a predictive manner to define relationships among variables.

Cluster analysis. Cluster analysis or clustering involves grouping data objects into clusters such that data objects in the same cluster have more in common with each other than with data objects in any other cluster (du Plessis and Botha, 2012). Cluster analysis is useful for identifying similarities among a data set (such as students or users) and grouping data into segments where multiple variables are related.

Software and Frameworks

R. An open-source, actively developed analytics tool increasingly adopted by colleges, universities, and data scientists.[1] Considered an alternative to commercial statistical programs such as SPSS and SAS, R is often preferred for its flexibility and customizability. To use R, it is helpful to have a working knowledge of UNIX and some programming knowledge. Extensive documentation is available,[2] and R programmer user groups meet regularly in many cities.

Apache Hadoop. A freely available open-source software solution designed to process huge data sets in a distributed computing environment. Its use as a data-storage solution extends beyond predictive analytics projects, but the advantage of using Apache Hadoop for big data is its scalability and its flexibility in growing a large data-mining store in a distributed network.[3] Unlike a traditional relational database that requires relations and schemas be defined before storing data, data stored in Hadoop's Distributed File System (HDFS) can be unstructured and don't require a schema (Dumbill, 2012). This means that as project parameters and analytics needs change, the data can be accessed in new ways without having to modify the structure of Hadoop's data storage. This flexibility is especially useful in a predictive analytics project, where variables and relationships are usually not known before the data is gathered.

NoSQL (Not Only SQL). These databases are similar to Hadoop's architecture in that they do not require predefined relations found in traditional relational databases. That these databases are referred to as "not only" SQL refers to the fact that SQL queries can be used on data stored in NoSQL databases. NoSQL databases are also flexible in terms of their ability to store documents (in a document-oriented architecture) as well as graph data (large sets of data points that can be represented by varying kinds of relationships, such as directories of people or map data). A popular example of a NoSQL database is MongoDB.[4]

LEARNING ANALYTICS

One of the most powerful ways for libraries to show the effectiveness of library use is by integrating library data with learning analytics initiatives. As systems are becoming increasingly capable of tracking how students engage with learning materials, "detailed learning activity can be used to predict how a student will perform in a future context, providing useful feedback to the student, the instructor, and the institution" (Oblinger, 2013). Libraries should be poised to lead learning analytics initiatives with the communities they serve to better understand and improve library services that have the greatest impact on learning.

Wolfgang Greller and Hendrik Drachsler (2012) provide a framework for understanding and designing learning analytics systems that enable more personalized learning. The authors advocate using learning analytics as both a reflective process (which focuses on "critical self-evaluation" of data sets and can suggest intervention strategies that improve learning) and a predictive process (which could use machine learning techniques to build learner profiles automatically and save teaching time for more personal interventions). Greller and Drachsler also caution that prediction in learning, whether data driven or by human intervention, must be considered carefully and respect privacy, as such predictions could limit a learner's potential. Using predictive models that improve processes and services and meet learners' needs more effectively should be the goal of predictive analytics projects—not making predictions about the performance of individual learners.

Katrien Verbert and colleagues (2012) further explore an emerging strand of research that emphasizes open and shareable learning and knowledge analytics (LAK). The practice of predictive analytics can be improved and refined by comparing and contrasting predictive models and outcomes established by other predictive analytics projects. Several organizations have emerged as public repositories to gather and share large data sets related to learning and knowledge. Repositories cited by Verbert and her colleagues include the Harvard Dataverse Network,[5] the PSCL DataShop,[6] and Data-Bib.[7] Libraries are also beginning to play an important role in the collection, publishing, sharing, and archiving of large data repositories, making experience with large data sets an increasingly important skill set for librarians (Huwe, 2014).

ETHICS AND PRIVACY

Libraries have a strong tradition of protecting patron privacy, and some methods of data mining and analytics can seem contrary to that tradition. Paul Schwartz (2011) argues that one of the most crucial phases of designing for predictive analytics is the phase during which an organization plans for collecting certain kinds of data. During this planning phase, it is essential that libraries consider ways to protect user privacy during data collection:

> Inform users. Always provide a mechanism for users to "opt out" of data gathering about their behavior and fully inform users about how data gathered on them will be used.
>
> Avoid personally identifying information (PID). Libraries should consider whether there is a compelling reason to associate personally identifying information (PID) with data gathered about user behavior. PID

can include information such as name, student number, social security number, phone number, physical address, IP address, or other data that can be used to identify a specific individual. It is often possible to anonymize data in such a way that a great deal of variables about users and their behavior can be gathered without personally identifying any individual users, or associating personally identifying information with behavioral data. In most cases, it is not necessary to store PID, as user behavior can often be tracked via cookies, session IDs, or anonymous tokens. Using these kinds of values to differentiate users can enable analysis of individual user behavior at an individual level without significantly compromising privacy.

Provide a benefit to users. The data gathered should always be meaningful and designed to benefit the users from whom it is gathered. Users should be informed about how they will benefit from their data, and every effort should be made to deliver those benefits to users in a timely manner. Careful planning with use cases that align with organizational goals is crucial to harnessing predictive analytics to improve user experience.

CONCLUSION

As Diana Oblinger (2013) writes, "Much of our data use has revolved around reporting on what has happened—in the past. Data use is moving to the predictive—to what is likely to happen." As systems become increasingly capable of tracking system interactions at a microlevel, it becomes increasingly important to identify goals for analytics and to have the knowledge and skills to assess the big picture in a sea of data. Understanding how predictive analytics technologies can benefit libraries and library users is increasingly becoming a crucial skill set as libraries seek new ways to improve accountability to stakeholders and improve services for library users. Data collection can be carefully planned to respect user privacy, while still creating meaningful predictive insights that can be deployed to improve library decision making on both a small and a wide scale.

NOTES

1. "The R Project for Statistical Computing," http://www.r-project.org/.
2. "An Introduction to R: Table of Contents," http://cran.r-project.org/doc/manuals/r-release/R-intro.html.
3. Hadoop, http://hadoop.apache.org/.
4. "MongoDB Architecture," MongoDB, http://www.mongodb.com/architecture.
5. Harvard Dataverse Network, https://thedata.harvard.edu/dvn.
6. PSCL DataShop, https://pslcdatashop.web.cmu.edu/.
7. DataBib, http://databib.org/.

REFERENCES

Alkhasawneh, R., and R. Hobson. (2011). "Modeling Student Retention in Science and Engineering Disciplines Using Neural Networks." *2011 IEEE Global Engineering Education Conference (EDUCON)*: 660–63.

Baepler, P., and C. J. Murdoch. (2010). "Academic Analytics and Data Mining in Higher Education." *International Journal for the Scholarship of Teaching and Learning*, 4.2: 4.

Dumbill, Edd. (2012). "What Is Apache Hadoop?" *O'Reilly Data*. O'Reilly, February 2.

du Plessis, S. A., and H. Botha. (2012). "Mining Wellness and Performance Data to Identify At-Risk First-Year Engineering Students." *Lecture Notes in Engineering and Computer Science*, 2197.1: 395–402.

Greller, W., and H. Drachsler. (2012). "Translating Learning into Numbers: A Generic Framework for Learning Analytics." *Educational Technology and Society*, 15.3: 42–57.

Han, Jiawei, and Micheline Kamber. (2006). *Data Mining: Concepts and Techniques*. Amsterdam: Elsevier.

Huwe, Terence K. (2014). "Big Data and the Library: A Natural Fit." *Computers in Libraries*, March 17+, 1 July.

Lauría, Eitel, Erik Moody, Sandeep Jayaprakash, Nagamani Jonnalagadda, and Joshua Baron. (2013). "Open Academic Analytics Initiative: Initial Research Findings." *Proceedings of the Third International Conference on Learning Analytics and Knowledge*: 150–54.

Maisel, Lawrence, and Gary Cokins. (2014). *Predictive Business Analytics: Forward-Looking Capabilities to Improve Business Performance*. Hoboken, NJ: Wiley.

Massis, Bruce. (2012). "Using Predictive Analytics in the Library." *New Library World*, 113.9/10: 491–94.

Oblinger, Diana G. (2013). "Analytics: Changing the Conversation." *EDUCAUSE Review*, 48.1: 48–49.

Oladokun, V. O., A. T. Adebanjo, and O. E. Charles-Owaba. (2008). "Predicting Students' Academic Performance Using Artificial Neural Network: A Case Study of an Engineering Course." *Pacific Journal of Science and Technology*, 9.1: 72–79.

Schmarzo, Bill. (2013). *Big Data: Understanding How Data Powers Big Business*. New York: Wiley.

Schwartz, P. M. (2011). "Privacy, Ethics, and Analytics." *IEEE Security and Privacy Magazine*, 9.3: 66–69.

Siegel, Eric. (2013). *Predictive Analytics: The Power to Predict Who Will Click, Buy, Lie, or Die*. Hoboken, NJ: Wiley.

Tufféry, Stéphane. (2011). *Data Mining and Statistics for Decision Making*. Chichester, UK: Wiley.

Verbert, K., N. Manouselis, H. Drachsler, and E. Duval. (2012). "Dataset-Driven Research to Support Learning and Knowledge Analytics." *Educational Technology and Society*, 15.3: 133–48.

Wu, James, and Stephen Coggeshall. (2012). *Foundations of Predictive Analytics*. Boca Raton, FL: CRC Press.

Chapter Two

Rethinking Service Models

Mobilizing Library Access for All Platforms

April Grey and Rachel Isaac-Menard

The library of the future is being reinvented and constructed, in the digital and brick-and-mortar worlds. As technology advances, it is essential that librarians consider upgraded and expanded service models that keep pace with the needs and habits of their patrons. It can no longer be assumed that users will walk in the front door, or even conduct library research via a desktop computer. The library of the future may well be visited on a mobile device. Therefore, librarians need to reach users where they are most active, and for many institutions, this means increasing online access points.

Technology enables libraries to remove access barriers, as it opens up a wider range of online options for users. Patrons are employing a variety of virtual platforms, and during this time of technology transition from desktops to mobile devices, it is important that library services display across desktop computers, laptops, tablets, and smartphones, seamlessly offering library resources searchable on all systems. This gives patrons "entering" the library on a desktop computer equal access to those on a smartphone or laptop.

Adding another layer of complexity, not every user will come into the virtual library at the same point, or begin by seeking out the library home page. Libraries must consider ease of access and multiple "entry" points to their systems for virtual patrons. To compete with other user-friendly information resources accessible on increasingly popular mobile technology, it is critical for libraries to create access points to resources and services in a similar way via icons. Users of all ages, particularly students, have come to rely more on these graphic indicators than on text directions.

Chapter 2

LITERATURE REVIEW

The technological revolution has affected and influenced libraries and their patrons. As recently as the late 1980s, patrons had to visit the library physically, or call or write a letter, to obtain the resources and services they required (Husain and Ansari, 2006, p. 43). At that time, library patrons entering the facility could search library holdings on the online public access catalog (OPAC), an experience that broadened in the early 2000s with the widespread use of personal computers, the Internet, and new software programs enabling access to library searches from home. Responding to this development, libraries increasingly migrated information online. Further technological advancements in library services have taken the form of online chat reference, digital libraries, and full-text electronic journal access, to name a few. Within the past twenty years, libraries have transitioned from traditional print correspondence to online features such as e-mail correspondence, web logs, wikis (websites on which users collaborate in creating the content), and social media platforms such as Facebook, Twitter, and Pinterest.

Libraries create online content with the patrons' interests in mind. However, resources that are intended to provide access can sometimes create barriers, due to the technology employed, software created exclusively for certain platforms, and the design of the interface itself. Patrons have to actively seek out the library content via the Internet, and they can accomplish this effectively only when they understand the technology, when they have access to the hardware needed (desktop, mobile phone, etc.), and when the information is presented in a logical, readily apparent way so they can search it intuitively.

In the academic setting, library services are often geared toward students as the primary user group, and services for students are often more fully developed than those for faculty (Dobbin et al., 2011, p. 10). The majority (85 percent) of students feel laptops are extremely important to their academic success. Of those students who work on mobile devices, 45 percent are on tablets, 37 percent are on smartphones, and 31 percent use e-book readers (Dahlstrom, Walker, and Dziuban, 2012, p. 24). As universities work to serve users who access their resources on current technology, with these statistics in mind, many are preparing for the next wave of technology as well (Johnson et al., 2014, p. 8).

These continually improving technologies can sometimes create barriers to access. For example, the seemingly uncomplicated task of downloading a quick response (QR) code reader can constitute a barrier to using the technology. A QR code is the black-and-white matrix barcode that contains information readable by the camera of a smartphone. In one study, the first barrier was smartphone ownership; the second barrier was the lack of an easy-access interface. The multiprocedure (multiclick) process was considered too time intensive. The students essentially rejected the QR code technology in favor of the traditional library resources (nonmobile). Even when a contest with a cash prize incentive was offered, the instances of students downloading the QR code reader onto their smartphones remained very low. Therefore, libraries should be cautious before fully committing to a particular solution due to the changing technological landscape and issues related to ease of use (Walsh, 2010, p. 61).

Many universities now use mobile technologies and create mobile-optimized versions of their websites for their patrons who use mobile devices (Dahlstrom, Walker, and Dziuban, 2012, p. 5). However, there is concern that students without smartphones are unable to take advantage of these access points. Cost and other restrictions are reasons students might lack access to a mobile device, and therefore integrating mobile technologies into the curriculum as the exclusive access point would not be appropriate (Chen and Denoyelles, 2013). It is less important to insist on cutting-edge technology than to understand how, where, and when students choose mobile technology and plan accordingly (Beckmann, 2010, pp. 160–61).

Another consideration relevant to access is where the library resources will reside online. Do library patrons seek entry to resources through a library home page, a university home page, or other site? One option gaining support is to integrate library guides into course management systems (CMSs; Lippincott, 2005, p. 58). Integrating resources into technology associated with the course will facilitate learning for all students (Beckmann, 2010, p. 162). At the same time, technology changes rapidly, and universities are exploring the use of mobile devices for access, especially as students migrate increasingly toward mobile technologies.

A report that concluded that resources must be built into a CMS also stated that "virtually any service a student uses on campus" could be integrated into a mobile application (app) to provide comprehensive student services. Offering the ability to reach a mobile-optimized library home page and library resource access points through smartphones and tablets will hopefully enhance the student experience with library resources (Johnson et al., 2014, pp. 8–9), as it has with other services.

When making changes for the overall mobile responsive design of the CMS, web developers should focus on student needs. University information technology (IT) departments are concentrating on apps for students that will combine all university services, in addition to social networking. These apps include admissions, financial aid, grades, billing, registration, and the CMS. The goal is to incorporate all university departments and services that contribute to student success. Web developers should be aware of the importance of design elements as well.

Overall, in an academic context, students comprise the largest library user group, and they seek scholarly sources to support research; they are not looking for the content the library presents on social media. This may factor in the "low use" of library social media sites that Kwabena Sekyere discusses, since students turn to social media for fun rather than research (2009, p. 26). Further, access to library resources via social media is a multiclick process. Patrons have to find the library on social media and then follow the library page. It would be preferable that they interact initially with the scholarly resources, rather than follow the social media.

New social media platforms are being created continuously, and librarians must identify and assess them for library suitability. For example, some libraries have abandoned their Facebook and WordPress sites in favor of Tumblr to keep up with the current trends. It can be assumed that new technologies will continue to emerge and might serve as ways to reach out to patrons online.

Seeking to facilitate the easiest and most comprehensive access for its student population, as part of a redesign of the campus library portal, Adelphi University Libraries studied its library resource usage statistics and considered the pitfalls identified through the professional literature. It was determined that students would most readily retrieve library services via the university CMS, Moodle, and the university portal, eCampus, access points available by both computer and mobile devices. It was also decided that the new access points would continue to focus on traditional academic library services that students require and request, incorporate graphics, and not include social media.

ECAMPUS

The eCampus service is the portal through which students access their university resources such as Moodle, class schedules, grades, financial aid, and various other university services. The eCampus product is built using the Liferay portal (http://www.liferay.com/), which is open source (free of charge and available to the general public for use, with an enterprise license). All changes to the library's eCampus page have to be approved and implemented by the university IT department. Although the library has input, it does not have total control over its pages. Formerly, the library section on eCampus was very minimal. It consisted of links to the library home page, biBLiOGraphy (the library's blog), and social media (Facebook and Twitter).

On the landing page, there was limited information about the library's resources, which focused more on the social media content. A basic link to the library home page, not customized to a particular user, it was experienced

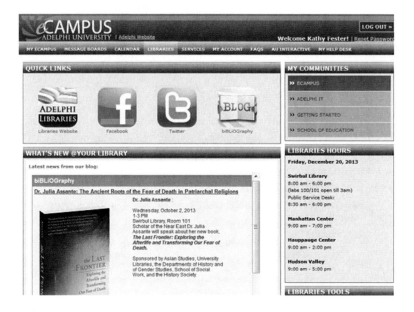

Figure 2.1. eCampus prior to 2014 changes.

in the same way by students or faculty, and there were no accommodations made for the needs of the various user groups.

MOODLE

Moodle is Adelphi University's course management system, or CMS, for students and faculty to facilitate online discussion and electronic document sharing. Faculty members are encouraged to post materials to this virtual classroom space and create a robust, interactive online experience for the students. Students turn in assignments through Moodle facets, retrieve their syllabi, and conduct classroom discussions. Previous to September 2013, Adelphi University Libraries did not have a presence on Moodle. Since a majority of courses are integrated into the Moodle platform, and students were accustomed to going to Moodle for academic needs and scholarly dialogue, the library designated it the opportune entry point for student access to library resources.

NEEDS ANALYSIS

Adelphi University Libraries utilized Google Analytics to obtain valuable data concerning student habits in accessing the library's resources, and this data was used to inform decisions on how to improve availability of its services. Aggregating diverse sets of data, the library created a snapshot of who sought out and used library resources and how they interacted with the library website to locate library materials. This snapshot indicated that the library had an access point to its resources (see figure 2.1) on the eCampus website that was not being used by the Adelphi community.

The data also revealed that many users went directly to the library home page. However, the library had determined the benefits of increasing the number of users coming to the library website from eCampus and Moodle. Because students were already accessing their other university services on eCampus and their courses on Moodle, they could authenticate once and gain access to library resources. This would streamline access by eliminating the need to go to another web page and reenter a username and password.

The library responded by implementing a major redesign of the website. This increased efficient and straightforward student access to the library resources via eCampus and Moodle. It also provided multiple access points to prevent students from getting discouraged and to reduce barriers to accessing library resources.

REDESIGN

eCampus

Adelphi University Libraries was approached by the university IT department to make changes to coincide with a university-wide redesign of eCampus. The library took advantage of this opportunity to improve its landing page on eCampus. It tasked the library's web services committee to set out a series of specific objectives. One of these was to separate users into three groups—faculty/administration, undergraduate students, and graduate students—and then customize eCampus accordingly. Using the new design, once an individual authenticates in eCampus, he or she is directed to one of the three user group service areas, depending on his or her designation.

Another goal was to guide user groups more effectively and quickly to the services and resources of relevance to them. For example, the faculty landing page now includes a link to media equipment requests, and the student landing page incorporates a link to library guides.

The library relied on usage statistics, as well as an internal survey, to determine the services and resources for the eCampus redesign. The committee surveyed faculty librarians to identify those provisions most and least used by each user group. The committee hoped that usage of certain offerings would increase once attention was drawn to them on eCampus.

After the committee determined which services and resources would be offered, they discussed design and information display elements. To attract student attention with the library landing page on eCampus, the committee elected to apply the visual concept of icons from mobile apps. Codes attached to each icon would enable the committee to track its usage, providing valuable data back to the library. Design considerations also included ease of recognition and shape, because the icons would have to display in proportion to the screen size, particularly important for mobile device users.

The committee examined the layout of the icons on a variety of popular mobile devices, including the Samsung Galaxy Tablet, iPad2, iPhone5, and a Nokia Lumia phone. Significantly, the various devices displayed different configurations of the icons. For example, the iPad shows five rows of four icons, whereas the Nokia phone displays three rows of five. The committee debated the ideal visual. The choices considered were three rows of five icons, three rows of four icons, two rows of five icons, and two columns of five icons. The committee's choice was three rows of five icons, primarily because this arrangement displayed properly on all of the mobile devices.

Having selected a display mode, the committee then tested a range of icons. The services for which icons had been created did not total fifteen. Therefore, the final display on the undergraduate and graduate pages shows two rows of five and one row of two icons (see figures 2.2 and 2.3). On the faculty/administration page, the third row shows three icons.

One of the major icon design challenges was to create a distinctive image to portray each service. The committee's first task was to convey the scope of library services and resources and the library's role on campus to the graphic designer. Options for icon design would be limited by the specific guidelines and requirements from the university IT department, which sought uniformity in the Adelphi University branding on eCampus.

The original icon concepts were drawn up by two library faculty members with backgrounds in artistic graphic design. The library created mockups, which were presented to the IT department. IT required the library to make changes to align with its branding specifications. The mockups were then presented to the graphic designer, who tried to accommodate the library's design while incorporating the requirements already in place for eCampus. Ultimately, the committee struck a compromise between the two design sets and collaborated with the graphic artist to finalize the icons.

Optimizing Moodle

The eCampus redesign project presented an opportunity to add library content to Moodle for both faculty and students. The committee opted to create a "library services" box in Moodle, sized at approximately three inches square. It determined the most useful information for Moodle and created a list of course- and subject-specific links. These links include the library website, contact information for the subject librarian, and the library guide.

Figure 2.2.   Faculty/administration eCampus landing page after redesign.

Another improvement was to add a link to library services and resources on the Moodle landing page to enable library faculty to convey information to instructors and adjuncts, as well as to remind seasoned faculty of the services the library offers. This link brings the faculty member to the library page that includes explanations on placing material for course reserve, providing library instruction forms, and borrowing equipment.

MARKETING

Marketing the finished product to the Adelphi community was an important component of the redesign effort. The committee used several approaches to convey updates about the new landing pages to library users.

When a revised version of eCampus was launched in January 2014, university IT sent out an e-mail to all faculty, staff, and students, informing them about the new website, including the major changes in the library services page. Faculty librarians received an internal e-mail explaining the updates and the use of icons. Students were alerted to the changes during library instruction sessions.

The library sent an e-mail blast to the Adelphi community about the new look to eCampus. The library also created a graphic about the eCampus redesign for its home page. This graphic was used on digital displays both

Figure 2.3. Graduate student eCampus landing page after redesign.

within the library and around campus. University IT also added a graphic to the main eCampus header.

The redesign to the look and use of Moodle was not as drastic, and the library believed it was sufficient for the individual subject librarians to inform the teaching faculty and students of the additions during their library instruction sessions.

CHALLENGES

The committee encountered multiple challenges throughout the eCampus redesign process. University IT placed constraints upon the library to create icons that conformed to IT's color and size requirements. Even with the help of the graphic designer, the committee had to generate multiple draft images and ultimately had to compromise on the final icons. The committee would have preferred to meet more frequently with the graphic designer to further explain the library services and resources that the images would convey.

Another challenge was managing a library web services committee whose members possessed a variety of technological abilities. Reaching a consensus was a slow process, because the committee had to have buy-in from all of the stakeholders, including the library web services committee, the graphic designer, and university IT. Scheduling conflicts often made it difficult for the entire committee to meet. Consequently, many decisions had to be made through e-mail, and committee members gave opinions and suggestions from attached screenshots, which was not ideal.

Furthermore, IT had allotted a short time line for the project. As a result, the committee could conduct only an internal survey of library faculty re-

Figure 2.4. Interlibrary loan icon progression from library idea to graphic artist interpretation to final graphic (from left to right).

garding eCampus, rather than a broad survey of students and teaching faculty. Another limitation of this tight time line was not being able to use Google Analytics thoroughly. Given more time, the committee would have conducted focus groups and additional testing with the different user groups.

LESSONS LEARNED

It is important to examine various access points to library resources and develop a plan of action to provide well-conceived and useful resources for various user groups. When working with other university groups, librarians need to communicate the library's services and resources and advocate for its needs. Often the library is coordinating with other departments that have their own objectives. With collective communication, librarians can collaborate effectively. For example, the committee, university IT, and the graphic designer joined forces to create icons that accurately convey visual messages about the library's resources.

Operating on a short deadline with many collaborators requires a great deal of patience and planning so that all participants feel they are involved and their opinions are being heard. Appointing a project manager who acts as lead contact internally and externally is critical to finalizing decisions and finishing projects.

Figure 2.5.

CONCLUSION AND FUTURE CONSIDERATIONS

One topic that Adelphi University Libraries can explore in the future is matching other access points to the redesigned eCampus. All library access points would then have similar icons, creating seamless and uniform service across platforms. The library is currently developing a mobile app to utilize these icons, and it plans to explore using them on the library web page as well. In addition, the library plans to conduct focus groups to determine whether students prefer an icon-based website to the current text-based website. Other libraries can use these ideas to create and implement icons to assist their users and integrate with mobile devices.

REFERENCES

Beckmann, E. A. (2010). Learners on the move: Mobile modalities in development studies. *Distance Education, 31.*2: 159–73.

Chen, B., and Denoyelles, A. (2013). Exploring students' mobile learning practices in higher education. *Educause Review Online.* Retrieved from http://www.educause.edu/.

Dahlstrom, E., Walker, J. D., and Dziuban, C. (2012). *ECAR study of undergraduate students and information technology.* Boulder, CO: Educause Center for Applied Research.

Dobbin, G., Dahlstrom, E., Arroway, P., and Sheehan, M. (2011). Mobile IT in higher education. *Educause Center for Applied Research, Research Report.*

Dowd, N. (2013, May 7). Social media: Libraries are posting, but is anyone listening? *Library Journal.* Retrieved from http://lj.libraryjournal.com/.

Fang, W. (2007). Using Google Analytics for improving library website content and design: A case study. *Library Philosophy and Practice,* 1–17.

Husain, R., and Ansari, M. A. (2006). From Card Catalogue to Web OPACs. *DESIDOC Bulletin of Information Technology, 26.*2: 41–47.

Johnson, L., Adams Becker, S., Estrada, V., and Freeman, A. (2014). NMC Horizon Report: 2014 Library Edition.

Lippincott, J. K. (2005). Net generation students and libraries. *Educause Review, 40.*2: 56–66.

Sekyere, K. (2009). Too much hullabaloo about Facebook in libraries! Is it really helping libraries? *Nebraska Library Association Quarterly, 40.*2: 22–27.

Walsh, A. (2010). QR Codes: Using mobile phones to deliver library instruction and help at the point of need. *Journal of information literacy, 4.*1: 55–65.

Chapter Three

Taming the Kudzu

An Academic Library's Experience with Web Content Strategy

Ian Demsky and Suzanne Chapman

For a long time, the University of Michigan (U-M) Library's website was like a garage stuffed with boxes labeled "KEEP." There was a lot of important stuff in there but also a lot that was old, broken, or no longer needed: links to automated teller machine locations for two local banks, a page with pictures of two beige campus phones, and a bevy of published "test" pages. It wasn't anyone's fault—it's just that it wasn't anyone's job to take the long view.

Academic libraries are just beginning to embrace the need to manage their web content more strategically. The emerging discipline of web content strategy has drawn attention to the consequences of allowing content to grow organically, with little oversight, over years or even decades. In the private sector, frustrating one's users can lead to a loss of sales to a competitor. But the stakes are also high for libraries. Library websites are increasingly becoming primary "places" for university faculty, students, and outside researchers to access materials, resources, and services. As Cushla Kapitzke (2001) puts it, "While still located in buildings, libraries are gradually transforming into dematerialized nodes of virtual, informational space that span oral, print, and digital cultures" (p. 451). This suggests the need for increased attention and resources devoted to better serving users' needs online, particularly given the rapid pace of change—in just one example of the new realities libraries face, higher education consultant Noel-Levitz (2013) found that 43 percent of students now report doing all of their web browsing on mobile devices.

The U-M Library is a large, complex, decentralized organization with roughly five hundred librarians and staff members spread across more than sixty units. When the library hired a full-time web content strategist in July 2013—one of the first such library positions in the country—its online eco-system included the following:

- roughly ten thousand pages of web content living within and outside of multiple content management systems;[1]
- about 180 people across the library with the power to create web content, largely operating autonomously in siloed units;
- no style guide or best practices guidance for content creators;
- no high-level oversight and curation; and
- no formal processes for approving new content, or for inventorying and evaluating existing content.

There was actually a higher degree of review required to place an item in the weekly internal newsletter than on the public-facing website, whose pages received more than 1.3 million unique visits in 2013.

As the new content strategist joined the User Experience (UX) Department's efforts to apply the principles of web content strategy within the library, it soon became clear that there were two distinct areas of concern: the challenging work of making the library's website more clear, consistent, and useful, and the human side of the equation—managing the required change within the organization. As Kathryn Deiss (2004) notes, many libraries are mature organizations that have well-established internal structures, work patterns, and institutional cultures that are resistant to change or disruption (p. 24). So it wasn't surprising that the UX Department experienced a mixed response to efforts to shape the quality of the library's web content and to set limits on what the organization should be willing to produce and maintain. But the UX Department couldn't just declare "content bankruptcy" and start from scratch. The department had to find a path forward that engaged the library's many stakeholders, while efficiently improving and modernizing the website to better serve users.

This brief chapter doesn't attempt to rearticulate the principles of web content strategy or how to create good web content. For guidance, see writings by Kristina Halvorson (2010), Sara Wachter-Boettcher (2012), Steve Krug (2006), and Janice Redish (2012). Instead, this chapter discusses lessons learned from the successes and challenges of trying to implement these principles within a large, decentralized library and offer a heuristic for considering the opportunities and tradeoffs inherent in three possible strategic alignments.

BACKGROUND

The U-M Library's web presence debuted in 1997. As the Internet Archive's Wayback Machine shows, at the time users were still encouraged to use a software program known as tn3720 or the telnet protocol to access Mirlyn, the library's catalog. Access via the web was newly available, but the online catalog was considered "an experimental version." Meanwhile, the home page provided a portal to general library information and a page of links to digital resources, but search-and-browse capabilities were listed as "Under Development" (University Library, 1997).

By 2013, the site had grown tremendously. Users from around the globe now generated more than 9.7 million page views while accessing library information, resources, and services on the main site, and an additional 5.7 million page views in the catalog. The library's online presence spanned not only the three thousand pages of content on the main website (built in the Drupal content management system [CMS]) but also nearly one thousand multipage research guides (in Springshare's LibGuides CMS),[2] about fifteen active subsites built in a soon-to-be-retired university platform called Site-maker, and numerous online exhibits created using the Omeka CMS as well as static HTML.

In that sixteen-year period, the library's web content mostly grew in an organic fashion—with many of the individual units and libraries that make up U-M Library maintaining their own websites until most were brought into a unified Drupal site in 2009. Since its inception, the library's web presence has expanded and changed based on the emerging needs of each unit, along with their employees' skill sets and available resources. If librarians in one library wanted to make a virtual tour of their facility, no one was going to try to stop them or ask hard questions about use cases, goals, plans for keeping the content up to date, or the expected return on investment. No one was going to come back later with usage statistics and suggest maybe it was time to archive and retire the project. Given a university and library culture strongly oriented toward decentralization, even the move to the Drupal framework, despite the continued support for near-complete author freedom, was seen by some as impinging upon the autonomy of the individual librarians and units.

As in many places, the library's longstanding attitude toward the web was that more was *more* and that there was really no harm in letting the website develop however individual units and librarians thought best. But as Rebecca Blakiston (2013) explains, "Unfortunately, few libraries predicted the content problems that this would create down the road. . . . Users visit our websites for content, but often what they ultimately find is poorly written, outdated, and duplicative content" (p. 176). From a review of the U-M Library's content as it stood in early 2013, the list could be expanded to include poor or missing metadata, internally focused content, low user-value content, disorganized content, orphaned pages not connected to any navigation pathway, and a host of overlooked "test" pages.

Rather than just being a mere annoyance, this kudzu-like proliferation of content leads to consequential difficulties:

- a poor signal-to-noise ratio that makes it hard for users to search the site efficiently;
- potential loss of credibility and trustworthiness with frustrated users;
- wasted time, effort, and opportunity costs when staff members spend valuable time creating and maintaining problematic or unnecessary content;
- general disorganization that makes it difficult for web specialists to improve the site's overall information architecture and navigation; and
- additional resource costs for web specialists to come back later and clean up faulty content.

One measure of how bloated the library's site had become can be seen in an initial tidy-up effort conducted by the UX Department in early 2013. When the department asked page owners simply to review their content to see if it was all still needed, authors ultimately unpublished or deleted 1,215 pages from the library's website—42 percent of published Drupal pages at the time! Ownership for 577 additional pages was reassigned, indicating that oversight had lapsed over another 20 percent of the site. It's worth noting, however, that this result required about sixty hours of project management: gathering and organizing information about each unit's content, e-mailing page authors, tracking changes in a spreadsheet, and nudging content owners—sometimes several times—as deadlines came and went.

As Halvorson points out, success on the web demands that content be treated as an integral core asset, rather than a secondary consideration (2010, p. 3). To work well, figuring out what to say cannot be a separate process from figuring out where content lives, what it looks like, and how it functions. Yet those within the library who had expressed feelings of dissatisfaction with the website and a desire for it to look and function better had rarely pointed to content as a major obstacle. The content issues were surprisingly invisible. The UX Department frequently heard complaints about the decision to move to the Drupal platform, demonstrating a conflation of the platform with the architecture the library had created in that platform and the content it had been populated with—including legacy content that had been portaged from previous versions of the site without review.

WEB CONTENT STRATEGIST ROLE

Enter the web content strategist. Halvorson defines web content strategy as "the practice of planning for the creation, delivery, and governance of useful, usable content" (2010, p. 32). That is, it delves into every aspect of the content life cycle with a focus, first and foremost, on helping *users* accomplish their goals. ("Users" primarily refers to key external users; in the library's case, U-M students, the faculty, the staff, and alumni, and secondarily the global public, along with the larger community of librarians at other libraries.) As Erin Kissane (2011) articulates, rather than providing a step-by-step blueprint, the discipline of content strategy rests on a series of core principles—namely, that content should be appropriate, useful, user centered, clear, consistent, concise, and supported. While the discipline, especially as it relates to the web, is relatively young, similar tenets have guided newspapers and other publishing operations for decades.

Whether web content strategy is the purview of an individual or a team, important aspects of the practice include the following:

- inventorying and understanding the existing content ecosystem;
- setting a vision and goals for the future;
- cleanup and improvement of existing content;
- creating guidelines, policies, and workflows for new content;
- determining publishing privileges, roles, and responsibilities;
- refining site navigation and organization (i.e., the relationships between various pieces of content);
- working to understand and meet user needs through testing and assessment;
- establishing and enforcing style guidelines and generally creating a consistent, professional voice across the website;
- planning for the ongoing maintenance, archiving, and retirement of content;
- prioritizing content work based on available resources;
- helping to conceive of and develop new projects and content areas;
- serving as a liaison between internal "clients" and web developers;
- establishing processes for resolving disagreements about content; and
- creating best practices and how-to documentation for content creators and helping to train them.

At the U-M Library, the web content strategist is deeply involved in each of these tasks, with support from the rest of the UX Department, the Web Systems Department, and a newly empowered team of nine web content coordinators, who serve as liaisons to the library's major internal divisions (more on the content coordinators below).

Moving from an organic, laissez-faire approach to a more strategic method of organizing and structuring web content can dramatically decrease the resources required to maintain content. At the same time, this shift allows organizations to adapt to important trends in web development: making content platform-agnostic to serve desktop, tablet, and mobile users; making content accessible to more users, including those with visual impairments and other disabilities; and taking advantage of the ability to associate related areas of content (Wachter-Boettcher, 2012).

A recent UX-initiated project to improve the library's Services for Patrons with Disabilities content exemplifies this less-is-more approach. Previously, accessibility information for individual libraries could be found both on each of seventeen individual library location pages and on a central Services for Patrons with Disabilities page. Not only were these entries duplicative, but also they were frequently inconsistent, and the pages—which often had different owners—had to be updated separately whenever information changed.

Under the new model, the content "lives" on each library's page and is merely linked to from the central page. This allowed the UX Department to delete about a dozen pages of duplicate content while decreasing the time and energy required for the content's upkeep. It is also worth noting that while updating and coalescing the accessibility information was a relatively straightforward task, the project required coordinating with about twenty people from library administration, library operations, and each of the individual library locations. Without a person or a group empowered to seek out and implement improvements across all of the organization's web content, this type of multiunit effort would likely never have happened.

In this way, content strategy can be seen as an integral component of user experience—alongside information architecture, user interface design, multiplatform planning, accessibility, and functionality (IBM, 2014). While there are many definitions of user experience that highlight the need to make content easier to find and use, the website Usability First describes it as "the totality of the experience of a user when visiting a website. Their impressions and feelings. Whether they're successful. . . . The extent to which they encounter problems, confusions, and bugs" (Usability First, 2014).

On an academic library's website, success is foremost equated with whether a user can accomplish their research tasks, such as finding an item in the catalog, accessing an electronic resource, or asking a reference question. The U-M Library's web analytics show that the next highest category of online activity revolves around finding information about the library's services: building locations, hours, study rooms, circulation activities, events and exhibits, and location-specific resources. Under a user-centered approach, the library should prioritize making high-value, high-impact tasks as simple and easy as possible. And the library should make sure that problems created by poorly managed content don't get in the way of core activities and the services it wants to promote. For example, prior to recent improvements, users who searched for information about the library's annual undergraduate research award were confronted by several pages of search results containing a confusing array of web pages and announcements, many with virtually identical titles; the main page for the awards program was lost in a sea of results. The UX Department was, however, able to reorganize, rearchitect, and consolidate the information so that the main page is now clearly distinguished and appears first in search results.

FREEDOM, EASE, QUALITY—PICK TWO

While the UX Department had tackled discrete content improvements in the past, the arrival of the web content strategist highlighted the tensions inherent in a single unit trying to instill new values and disrupt long-established work practices within the institution. No matter what approach was taken, it would come with tradeoffs. The department considered three common strategic approaches for managing web content. These ranged from continuing the library's historical hands-off approach to a model that centralized editorial control and essentially "locked down" the site. At the time of this writing, the organization is in the process of a slow transition toward a middle ground that relies on distributed control and a system of checks and balances.

As the UX Department saw it, the issue boiled down to a slightly tweaked version of the classic project management triangle, which says that time, cost, and scope must always be weighed and balanced—and that one can never maximize all three of those elements at the same time (McGhee and McAliney, 2007, p. 23). Or in a more informal phrasing, you have to pick two: fast, cheap, or good. You can have fast and cheap, but the results won't be good; you can have cheap and good, but it will take more time; or you can have fast and good, but it will cost more.

Reimagined for a web content strategy context, the authors posit that one can maximize only two of the following aspects of content creation and management simultaneously: author freedom, overall quality, and speed/ease of publishing. As discussed below and displayed in figure 3.1, the three possible configurations each come with opportunities and tradeoffs.

Wild West Model

If authors are given complete freedom and a premium is placed on removing barriers to quick publishing, then quality will suffer (as those 1,215 unneeded pages showed).

Figure 3.1.   Aspects of content creation and management.

Checks and Balances Model

If an organization chooses to give authors a high degree of freedom but establishes workflows (e.g., an approval process, UX consulting on major initiatives, editorial review prior to publication, graduated levels of publishing privileges, regular assessment, and weeding) to ensure high quality, then speed and ease will be diminished.

Specialist Led

And lastly, if quality and speed are given priority—namely, by having experienced communications and web professionals write, edit, post, and manage the bulk of the content—then the freedom of individual librarians and units to create content will be curtailed. An extreme version of this approach was implemented by the University of Virginia Library in 2012, when it unveiled a new website that shrank content from fourteen thousand pages to sixty (Seal, 2012). Less drastic models are also possible. During a website redesign, the Richland Library in Columbia, South Carolina, turned the top two levels of site content into the sole purview of their marketing and web staff but allowed more freedom for others to create content deeper in the site (Coulter, 2014).

Which two points of the triangle an organization chooses to maximize will likely depend on its relative size and complexity, its organizational values, and its appetite for hiring, training, or reallocating staff (see the appendix for a closer look at the three configurations and potential ways to mitigate the limitations of each). For the U-M Library, the Wild West Model was becoming increasingly untenable. And as efficient and simple as the high-control model might sound in the abstract, the UX Department knew the approach would not work without a major cultural shift within the library. So the path forward followed the middle model, one that still places a high premium on author freedom and independence but aims to improve quality by instituting additional oversight, coordination, and review—even though this somewhat diminishes the speed and ease of publishing.

WEB CONTENT COORDINATOR ROLE

While the library had slowly been moving in this direction for some time, the shift in approach might formally be dated from the formation of a web content coordinator (WCC) group, which began as a six-month pilot in November 2013. Cochaired by the web content strategist and the head of the UX Department, the group consists of representatives from each of the library's major divisions. Members were tasked with two main functions: first, to serve as a liaison to their divisions—guiding content creation and maintenance, communicating about new web content policies and high-level strategy, and ensuring that content meets newly articulated guidelines and best practices; and second, to work together on library-wide and cross-divisional issues, providing division-level feedback to the UX Department and the WCC group, and serving as a first-line appeals body for disagreements.

The group met weekly, alternating between regular, agenda-based meetings and optional sessions that could be set aside for individual web content work or smaller discussions of emergent issues. Meetings usually focused on broad topics, such as discussions of policies and oversight roles for the new library blogging platform, or were set aside for trainings on aspects of the larger web strategy. The UX Department cochairs also worked with the WCCs one-on-one to help prioritize projects within their division and to troubleshoot any technical or political problems they encountered. The web content strategist worked closely with individual coordinators on larger-scale projects, such as the development of a new information architecture for collections content and the migration of a large, newly acquired unit to the library's web space from multiple independent websites. Over the course of the pilot, the group had to negotiate uncertainties about coordinators' authority within their divisions, when and how the UX Department should guide or manage their efforts, and how to balance the role's needs with all of the coordinators' regular job duties.

Meanwhile, it was quickly evident that the coordinators' positions as "insiders" within their divisions—their relationships with upper-level managers and with their peers, along with their knowledge of the terrain—gave them additional leverage and helped to make every area of the library a genuine partner in the future of the website. Requests for content improvements were no longer the purview of the UX Department but part of the work of the division itself. And for the UX Department, sharing the concern and workload for web content among eleven people instead of two provided some welcome relief.

Over the course of the pilot, the coordinators tackled projects large and small, on their own and in coordination with each other and the UX Department. Despite the addition of several areas of content (along with the steady and continuous growth of events, announcements, and news items), their efforts led to a 12 percent reduction in content on the main Drupal website. At the end of six months, the pilot was deemed successful, and the WCC role was formalized with the support of each division's associate university librarian.

In a postpilot update shared with division leadership, the UX Department articulated the following premises under which the web effort would proceed:

- It is important to have a public web presence that presents high-quality, high-value content to support the mission of the library and help users to get their work done (and which is organized and presented in a user-focused way, not according to the library's organizational chart).
- Content creation isn't a one-time effort—content needs ongoing management, including regular evaluation and updating, and removal when the content is no longer needed.
- If a piece of content is worth having, it's worth doing right.
- Content isn't easy to "do right"—it takes an understanding of the underlying informational context and holistic needs of the website, plus expertise (e.g., facility with the technical infrastructure, plus an understanding of a user-centered approach, writing for the web, style guidelines, and potential accessibility issues).
- These aren't abilities that every content creator can be expected to have—creating professional-quality web content is a specialized skill, not unlike other specialized areas within the library such as instruction, reference, publishing, or cataloging.
- Given the complexity of "doing it right," the UX Department and web content coordinators should be a partner in all nontrivial web efforts across all library divisions.

Upon reflection, the pilot was successful in several ways: In the main, the web content coordinators embraced their role and were quick to recognize the importance and complexity of creating high-quality web content. They responded to divisional needs as they arose, and most were proactive about investigating and initiating solutions to existing problems. The group dynamic also helped improve communication, connections, shared vision, and holistic problem solving, and fostered a more collaborative spirit across divisions—though there is still work to be done. Moreover, their ability to support the needs of their divisions helped free up the UX Department to channel more effort into larger-scale improvements. The group also received positive feedback from several areas that were enthusiastic about the additional guidance, help improving their pages, and greater involvement in the web space.

Still, the initiative was not without its challenges: the WCC role was not equally accepted and supported across the internal divisions, which led to less success in some areas. Even though the creation of the WCC group was able to focus far more time and effort on web content than ever before, needs in some areas still outpaced available resources. Sometimes content creators within the divisions were slow to accept the new checks and balances, opting not to coordinate with their WCC on new efforts, or waiting until work was nearly complete before doing so. There also continue to be questions of authority, as well as uncertainty about when WCCs should be free to make decisions unilaterally and when they need to solicit consensus, when they need to defer to content creators and/or division leadership, and when they were free to override them.

FROM THEORY TO PRACTICE

As the UX Department and the WCCs became more active in cleaning up existing content and guiding new projects, the group found that despite efforts to communicate underlying intentions and rationale, there was still confusion within the library about what the group was trying to accomplish and why. Some content creators maintained the expectation that they would continue to have full autonomy and editorial control. Several efforts experienced some pushback or lack of engagement from both staff and managers. There were also questions of how to best communicate the new strategic approach internally given the lack of full internal alignment.

This was not entirely unexpected. Wachter-Boettcher reminds us that new content strategies can be extremely difficult to implement in large, complex organizations, as they can mean the disruption of long-standing work patterns, changes to power dynamics, insistence on higher standards of quality, limits on previous autonomy, and new forms of collaboration (2012, pp. 192–200). Such responses are also anticipated by the principles of change management developed in the corporate world to factor in the "human side" of major changes to organizational structures or work processes. As Marcus Gonçalves (2007) puts it, "Any fundamental change within the organization requires the generation and effective deployment of a culture that embraces change and the *need for change*" (p. 9, emphasis added). Key elements of change management he outlines include the following:

- articulating the formal case for change;

- beginning with the leadership team and engaging key stakeholders and leaders;
- having the leadership team speak with one voice and present a clear vision;
- going beyond tacit "buy-in" and creating ownership by letting employees identify problems, craft solutions, and share responsibility for improvements;
- communicating and reinforcing key messages;
- addressing culture explicitly and modeling and rewarding the new behaviors; and
- articulating how change will benefit the individual employee as well as the organization. (pp. 45, 77–81)

With these principles in mind, the UX Department and WCCs continue to work on communicating the strategic vision with the library—through newsletter items, blog posts, training sessions (e.g., "Tips for Writing for the Web"), and day-to-day interactions—along with ongoing engagement of library leadership, and attempts to foster more self-directed efforts at the unit level.

It is clear in hindsight that changes could have been better communicated at the outset of the shift toward a more strategic approach to the website. Yet the UX Department felt it had taken reasonable measures. The WCC pilot had the explicit support from the heads of each division—who were giving up a portion of an employee's time for the effort. It was also announced in the library's internal newsletter and explained in more detail on the intranet. Additionally, the UX Department believed the (successful) end of the pilot would be a better time for a more formal announcement of support from leadership. Several changes in library leadership were also under way during this time period, which complicated matters.

Learning from these initial efforts, however, the UX Department and WCCs later sought more explicit buy-in from leadership for a massive content cleanup of the library's research guides in preparation for migration to a new platform. One of the WCCs from the Learning and Teaching division put together a short presentation for the executive leadership team and, with their sign-off, also gave the presentation to senior managers. Managers, in turn, reinforced the importance of the initiative with their staff. Responsibility for the first round of review and cleanup was placed in the hands of each unit. Having the weight of the initiative cascade down through successive layers of the organization was far more effective than previous, far smaller efforts to work with guide authors individually. Over a six-week period, the initiative led to the retirement of 368 guides, more than a third of the total.

Another area in which the UX Department and WCC group discovered change needed to be managed was communication with general library staff.

One manager recently confided that the WCCs were seen as having a default position of saying "no" to requests for new web content, thus alienating some staff. Unfortunately, it's likely that a response that starts with asking questions—about a proposed piece of content's goals, audience, and relationship to existing content—is seen as a critique that will lead to a "no." While it is true that the UX Department believes that there is too much content on the library's website and that streamlining it will benefit users, the department needs to figure out how to better communicate that this interrogative approach is necessary. Proposals for new content provide an opportunity to look at their impact holistically. For example, the department recently received a request to update information about remote access to the library's electronic resources. There was no doubt that the library's current content needed to be improved. UX could have just put new language on the existing page, but by asking questions and looking at the information in a broader context, the department concluded that a constellation of about ten related pages needed updating too, to make the content easier to find and use.

Another area of potential misalignment is the strong sense of ownership and attachment to content by librarians and other content creators. In part, as Blakiston points out, this could be due to web content's role in highlighting technology skills and workplace contributions (2013, p. 176). It's far easier to demonstrate productivity by pointing to new pages or research guides than to deleted or merely well-maintained content!

Libraries also lack an editorial culture where content production and management is viewed as a collective rather than a personal effort. The web content strategist came from the journalism world, where content was subject to a formal editorial hierarchy and was understood to serve the needs of the publication as a whole. News stories have to be pitched and green-lighted and then are subject to one or more layers of editing prior to publication. It would not be unusual for a perfectly good news story to be cut in half at the last minute to make space for a late-breaking item. But there's no precedent for the role of an editor at the U-M Library—someone who might say, "Let's merge these two similar research guides," "I think we need to get to the point quicker in this item," or "I think this content has outlived its usefulness." For the UX Department, this has been a slow process of negotiation, and both the web content strategist and the WCC group are still feeling out the right level of editorial authority to exert in different contexts.

Similarly, there isn't always agreement about what constitutes high-value or high-priority content. Many units are eager to create content to promote their successes within and outside the institution: for example, grants, awards, publications, and unit histories. From a UX Department perspective, these offer only secondary value to core users—namely, university students, faculty, and staff—and the time and energy might better be spent on improvements that will benefit a much larger portion of the library's user base.

But the department is also very cognizant that these content areas are important to many librarians, and by deprioritizing this type of content, there is a risk that large portions of the organization will feel that the website doesn't meet their needs. This not only has the potential to sow resentment within the organization but also makes rogue projects outside of the CMS more likely. Thus, the UX Department has articulated a set of principles for web content that can be pointed to when disagreements over value and priority inevitably arise:

- starting with user needs and building in assessment;
- focusing attention on high-use, high-value content;
- keeping things simple to ensure sustainable, scalable, and extensible content;
- taking a holistic "one library" view, rather than letting the organizational chart dictate structure;
- designing and building for everyone, including meeting or exceeding accessibility standards; and
- embodying the twenty-first-century library by presenting ourselves as a unique and important campus resource for an array of services and expertise.

The UX Department and WCCs also try, whenever feasible, to offer alternatives to "permanent" web pages—which was the impetus behind the library's new blogging platform and which undergirds discussions of a possible "public intranet," which could house organization-focused content separately from user-focused content.

WHERE WE'RE HEADING

Ultimately the library needs a new website—one with a better search interface and cleaner overall design and one that is accessible to people with disabilities, responsive for mobile users, and architected around meeting users' primary needs. It should better support and guide both novice and expert users, while remaining flexible enough to shift and grow with whatever the next wave of technological change will bring.

The UX Department sees the current work—on the website and within the organization itself—as laying the groundwork for this next iteration of the library's online presence. The more content problems that can be solved now, the fewer there will be to tackle later. The more UX continues to communicate its vision and the need for change within the library, the more ownership might be fostered across the organization. UX aims to open channels for talking about what is working and not working for individuals, units, and the library as a whole. And if all goes well, there will be a better understanding throughout the organization that this type of librarianship is vital to the organization's continued success and relevance, and that it requires a shared vision, dedicated resources, skilled labor, and coordinated curation.

APPENDIX

Wild West

Control style: diffuse
Maximized: freedom, speed/ease
Suffering: quality

Pros:

- Individual librarians and units are empowered to create content around their own needs and interests.
- There are no barriers to publishing, and it is easier to meet emergent and niche needs.
- Resources required to produce and maintain content are spread across the organization.

Cons:

- No one is looking out for the whole.
- Quality is inconsistent. A significant portion of web content may not be clear, findable, useful, valuable, credible, or accessible.
- It does not acknowledge that professional-quality content, especially on the web, is a specialized skill.

Ways to mitigate downsides:

- Good documentation: best practices, style guide, and how-to instructions
- Training for authors
- Additional support resources for content creators, for example, web committee, UX Department, and web content strategist.

Checks and Balances

Control style: distributed
Maximized: freedom, quality
Suffering: speed/ease

Pros:

- Authors retain a high degree of freedom, but a review process ensures best practices and style guidelines are followed; it raises questions about content prior to publication; and it ensures that new content meshes with the larger context of the site.
- Policies for content creation and governance can be established.
- Quality is consistent.
- Attention is paid to usability and accessibility issues.
- It is easier to be "future ready."
- It can go beyond ex post facto review toward more front-end planning and coordination.

Cons:

- Approval process for new content and review prior to publication creates a barrier to immediate publishing.
- Approvers/reviewers and authors might disagree about content—including whether a particular piece is necessary.
- It requires dedicated resources, for example, full- or part-time attention from a web committee, UX Department, web content strategist, or web content coordinators embedded within units.

Ways to mitigate downsides:

- Change management practices.
- Introduce formal adjudication process for handling disagreements.
- Ensure good documentation, for example, best practices, style guide, and how-to instructions.
- Provide training for authors.
- Use regular assessment to help guide decision making.

Specialist Led

> Control style: centralized
> Maximized: quality, speed/ease
> Suffering: freedom

Pros:

- Top-level, priority, and core content (at a minimum) is created by professionals with backgrounds in communications, marketing, or web content—ensuring consistent, high-quality content that reflects positively on the organization and that is geared toward meeting user needs.

- Dedicated, skilled resources are available to tackle important areas of need and emergent issues.
- Content can be produced faster and is higher quality.

Cons:

- Freedom to create content is greatly diminished. Librarians lose this opportunity to build technology skills and to include web pages in their portfolios.
- Specialists may act as a bottleneck, requiring prioritization of content efforts. Units with lower priority content may be frustrated by having to wait.
- Units/librarians and specialists might disagree about content—including whether a particular piece is necessary—requiring both a clear organizational vision and an adjudication process.
- It requires fairly significant dedicated resources.

Ways to mitigate:

- Allow librarians and staff to create content at lower levels within the site hierarchy—with or without additional training and/or a formal editorial review process.
- Align internal resources so that the requisite resources are available to meet the actual demand for web content.
- Hire interns from journalism, communications, or similar programs on campus.

NOTES

1. The library's web space also includes several independently managed sister sites and more than 250 digital collections whose content falls outside of the scope of this discussion; they are not included in usage statistics presented here.

2. As of February 2014, according to a Springshare LibGuides Community analysis retrieved from http://libguides.com/community.php, U-M ranked number 18 in number of published guides among 2,696 higher education institutions, with more than 7.5 times more guides than the average institution.

REFERENCES

Blakiston, R. (2013). Developing a Content Strategy for an Academic Library Website. *Journal of Electronic Resources Librarianship, 25*(3), 175–91.

Coulter, K. (2014, April 9). The Ideal User Experience for Library Websites. *Prezi.com.* Retrieved June 21, 2014, from http://prezi.com/.

Deiss, K. J. (2004). Innovation and Strategy: Risk and Choice in Shaping User-Centered Libraries. *Library Trends, 53*(1), 17–32.

Gonçalves, M. (2007). *Change Management: Concepts and Practice.* New York: ASME Press.

Halvorson, K. (2010). *Content Strategy for the Web.* Berkeley, CA: New Riders.

IBM. (2014). Customer Facing Solutions Approach. Retrieved June 21, from http://www-03.ibm.com/.

Kapitzke, C. (2001). Information Literacy: The Changing Library. *Journal of Adolescent and Adult Literacy, 44*(5), 450–56.

Kissane, E. (2011). *Elements of Content Strategy.* New York: A Book Apart.

Krug, S. (2006). *Don't Make Me Think! A Common Sense Approach to Web Usability.* 2nd ed. Berkeley, CA: New Riders.

McGhee, P., and McAliney, P. (2007). *Painless Project Management: A Step-by-Step Guide for Planning, Executing, and Managing Projects.* Hoboken, NJ: Wiley.

Noel-Levitz. (2013). 2013 E-Expectations Report: The Impact of Mobile Browsing on the College Search Process. Retrieved June 21, 2014, from https://www.noellevitz.com/.

Redish, J. (2012). *Letting Go of the Words: Writing Web Content that Works.* 2nd ed. Waltham, MA: Morgan Kaufmann.

Seal, R. (2012, June 12). From 14,000 Pages to 60: Library Unveils Website Redesign. *UVA Today.* Retrieved June 21, 2014, from http://news.virginia.edu/.

University Library, University of Michigan. (1997, June 5). Home page. Retrieved June 21, 2014, from http://web.archive.org/web/19970605114203/http://www.lib.umich.edu.

Usability First. (2014). Glossary: Customer Experience. Retrieved June 21, from http://www.usabilityfirst.com/.

Wachter-Boettcher, S. (2012). *Content Everywhere: Strategy and Structure for Future-Ready Content.* Brooklyn, NY: Rosenfeld Media.

Chapter Four

Hollywood in the Library

Librarians and Video Production

Laura A. Staley

Librarians have always been creators of content, including brochures, bibliographies, information skills curriculum, and displays. Contemporary librarians have added a new format to their instructional and marketing toolkits. Today they are video makers as well. Here are two examples:

1. Seattle Public Library's 2014 Summer of Learning trailer: Upbeat music plays. A narrator tells us that the Seattle Public Library is doing something different this year with their summer reading program. On a black screen we see the title "2014 Summer of Learning—Zone In! Explore, Create, Connect." Dr. Mr. Will, a bespectacled man in a white lab coat, announces that he has decided to take his time machine to the future to get some answers. We see him with his cardboard box labeled "Time Machine" waving his arms against a vivid blue and pink psychedelic background as he travels into the future. After some brief worry about disturbing the space-time continuum, Dr. Mr. Will and his future self decide to try ten of the Zone In activities, right now. They are shown doing "3. Lego Balloon Car," "4. Straw Kazoo," "7. Typewriter + Poem," and "10. Bug-Bots!!!" Dr. Mr. Will and his future self jump for joy in front of a whiteboard. The words "Explore, Create, Connect" appear below them. The music swells. "2014 Summer of Learning—Zone In! spl.org/summeroflearning" appears on a black background as the video ends. YouTube: https://www.youtube.com/watch?v=CeCkEHyhf0M

2. "Renewing RTC Library Books Online" screen-capture video. "Renewing RTC Library Books Online" shows below the Renton Techni-

cal College (RTC) logo. The next screen shows the RTC Library home page. The voice-over narration tells the viewer that RTC library books can be renewed online. The cursor clicks on the "Library Catalog" link and then on the "My Account" link. Viewers are shown how to enter their ID and last name to log into their account. The checked-out books are displayed, and the book to be renewed is selected with the mouse. The Request Renewal button is clicked. The cursor moves to highlight the new due date. Viewers are told that this will only work if the item is not already overdue and that for overdue items they should contact the library. RTC Library contact information is displayed on the screen and narrated in the voice-over. YouTube: https://www.youtube.com/watch?v=sBmh2Y9_9L8andfeature=youtu.be

Librarians create videos for many purposes. Videos introduce patrons to library geography, services, rules, and resources. Videos are used to teach patrons to use the library catalog to find a book, or databases to find articles, how to navigate the library website, how to find and retrieve course reserves, and how to use scanners and copiers. They are used to teach patrons how to begin their research, how to log into the library databases from off campus, and how to request interlibrary loan. They teach how to read a citation and how to use software to create new bibliographies (Henrich and Prorak, 2010, p. 665). They can be used to introduce new books, new programs, and new staff (Buczynski, 2009, p. 42).

Library videos can be elaborate live-action minifilms, such as the Seattle Public Library video, animations, or a simple sequence of screen captures, like the Renton Technical College video. They can be short or long. They can be produced by professional video-production staff, librarians training on a new tool, or a classroom of communications students collaborating with their campus library.

THE PROS AND CONS OF MAKING A VIDEO

Video Pros

Videos offer information and instruction to patrons who can't or won't come to the library. In 2013, about half of U.S. adults aged sixteen and over used a public library—which means that half did not (Zickuhr, Purcell, and Rainie, 2014). The number of college students who don't visit their libraries is considerably smaller; 75 percent of college students visit their libraries "frequently" or "occasionally" (Enis, 2012). On the other hand, in 2013 78 percent of Americans watched or downloaded Internet videos (Purcell, 2013). Videos allow the library to reach most patrons where they can be found—on the web. And patrons who would never otherwise come to a library might be encouraged to visit if they believe there are systems in place to help them.

Videos also work for patrons who use the library but are unwilling to approach library staff. There are many reasons people won't approach librarians: because patrons don't want to bother the librarian, because they are embarrassed to ask about something they feel they should already know, or because they don't know how to ask the question they need answered. Videos created to answer short, specific queries can help these patrons answer their questions quickly, without requiring them to admit that they don't know something. The act of finding and using the videos should increase their confidence in their information-seeking prowess as well—and the confidence that library systems are understandable and navigable can also be useful.

Videos offer twenty-four-hour-a-day instruction. Most libraries have the resources to staff a reference desk during peak hours, and some can even offer reference assistance during the late night. But very few libraries can offer round-the-clock help by librarians who are experts in what their particular library offers. Videos can teach patrons to craft an effective search, find a journal article in a database, or put an item on hold even when the library is closed. In these times when demand is increasing and budgets and staff are decreasing, videos can take up some of the instructional slack.

Patrons expect most web pages to have active content. Meeting their expectations by using multimedia allows libraries to teach patrons important information in an anticipated format. It also encourages patrons to think of the library as a source of up-to-date technology (Buczynski, 2009, p. 42).

Marketing the library means competing with dozens of other entities all vying for a patron's attention. Most librarians can't bring a glee club or a flashing marquee with them, but videos allow libraries a variety of tools—including songs, eye-catching graphics, and attention-getting characters—to engage the attention of their patrons.

For academic librarians, videos also are a good way to reach the faculty. It can be relatively easy to reach students. Most campuses have freshman orientations or tours where students are taken to the library. Many schools require a writing class that will traditionally include a visit to the library, or a visit to the classroom by the librarian. There is often no similar mechanism for introducing new instructors to the library. This is especially true when the instructor is an adjunct. Adjunct training can be limited to directions to the copy machine and a URL for the website of the online class grade book. They might never be introduced to the library and its resources. This is not an insignificant problem. It is reported that over half of college instructors are adjuncts (National Center for Education Statistics, 2014). But videos—especially ones created for instructors—can solve this problem. For example, librarians at California State University–Northridge (CSU Northridge) created a series of one-minute videos intended to reach these faculty (Martin, 2012, p. 592). The topics covered included a library tour, the library's reserve and interlibrary loan services, and specialized services such as embedded librarians in the school's learning management system (Martin, 2012, p. 593).

Videos facilitate the flipped classroom. Videos can be used to teach basic tasks and give librarians more time to teach complicated skills. The more time librarians spend teaching patrons to log into library databases or find a book, the less time they have to teach the patron to hone a search statement or use a bibliography. Librarians who are scheduled to present to an English 101 class can assign one or two brief videos—for example, an introduction to the library and a tutorial on logging into the online databases—and then spend valuable class time working on more sophisticated matters such as identifying bias in a source or determining which database will give them the articles they need.

Videos can be replayed as many times as necessary. Patrons can watch them multiple times to understand the information. This is especially useful for English-as-a-foreign-language patrons who are dealing with vocabulary issues as well as unfamiliarity with library systems. Videos with both narration and captioning are doubly useful in this respect, giving practice in library skills, pronunciation, and reading in one neat package. Given the limits of reference desk staffing and instructor and classmate patience, this is one place where videos are clearly superior to in-person instruction.

Screencast videos can be custom made for an audience of one. The University of Lincoln in the UK made short videos to follow up on individual phone-call requests for help. Their videos, recorded on Jing, showed how to log into databases, search for journal articles, and do other online tasks. The URL for the Jing video was mailed to the students (Mansfield, 2010, p. 17).

Video Cons

Database interfaces and library policies change regularly. Unexpected changes in resources can make the video out of date, even during the production process (Gravett and Gill, 2010, p. 69). To continue to be relevant, the videos need to be updated to reflect these changes (Bowles-Terry, Hensley, and Hinchliffe, 2010, p. 19). A useful part of planning a video might include researching how long the content will remain relevant—but that information isn't always available (Henrich and Prorak, 2010, p. 673).

Videos require an ongoing marketing campaign. They cannot be made, mounted on the web, and then ignored. If the cost is to be recouped, patrons, librarians, and faculty need to be reminded regularly where they are and what they offer. In schools, the student body changes every year, and the school staff might turn over almost as often. This means that libraries need to continue to market their videos every quarter.

Videos always take more time to create than librarians anticipate. Most accounts of creating library videos mention this fact. Some have reported that the process took twice as long as they originally forecast (Gravett and Gill, 2010, p. 69; Majekodunmi and Murnaghan, 2012, p. 10). This is especially true if this is the first video the library has created.

The more complicated the project is, the more likely it is to take longer than scheduled. A short screencast, made with screen-capture software, and little if any narration, might only require one or two recordings. More ambitious efforts involving live actors, music, and narration will inevitability take longer. Scripts will require repeated rounds of editing. It will take longer to collect the equipment and book the locations than planners expect. Shooting the footage and dealing with light and sound issues and actors' schedules will take longer than anticipated. Adding narration and graphics will be more complicated than novices imagine. There could be delays in testing the final product and putting it on the web.

More time equates to more cost. Even if that cost is only in librarian release time, it is still time that could have been used doing something else. CSU Northridge's one-minute videos were estimated to take twenty-five to thirty-five hours for each member of the three-person team, including scripting, production, and postproduction work (Martin, 2012, p. 595).

Videos need to be carefully designed to engage patrons. There is no point in creating a video that patrons will turn off after the first fifteen seconds. This is less a problem for short skills-training segments, such as how to search the catalog, than it is for longer videos.

Videos need to be accessible to as much of the library's population as possible. As many as 15.6 percent of the world's population has a disability (Oud, 2011, p. 133). It is useful to design supporting materials to make sure that everyone can use this new resource. Supporting materials could include voice-over narration, captions, and transcripts. These will take time to create and will require space to house on a server.

Videos will not answer all of the questions patrons have on a subject. Many people learn better when they interact with another person. Some will always prefer to have a staff member show them how to log onto the library website rather than watch a video. A certain percentage of library patrons simply need human interaction, and no video can provide this.

When librarians are contemplating creating a video, they should consider all of these factors. They may also want to inquire if there are local government or school policies in place requiring approval of scripts, design constraints, and other restrictive requirements that could affect their work. Librarians work in a complex environment, where many human, institutional, and political restraints apply. When deciding to create a video, they will need to consider these factors as they begin the planning process.

PLANNING THE VIDEO

The process for creating a video usually involves five stages:

1. The decision stage
2. The video-planning process
3. The video-creation process
4. The video-editing process
5. The marketing process

The two most important parts of the video-creation process are the decision stage and the planning process. Careful planning will avoid problems with resources, finances, institutional barriers, and the ultimate usefulness of the videos. Because they are so important, they can be the longest part of the process. But time spent in the first two steps will save time in the expensive shooting or recording process (Henrich and Prorak, 2010, p. 673). The decision-making stage should include answering these questions:

- What do we intend to teach?
- Is a video the best way to teach it?
- Has anyone already made this video?
- If a video that we create is the best solution, what kind of video do we need?
- What will it cost?
- What are the administrative requirements? Script permission? Filming permission? Photo/filming releases?
- Where will we store this video?
- What internal resources do we have to make this video?
- What external resources can we access to make this video?

What Do We Intend to Teach?

What part of the library's instructional strategy is this going to support? Most libraries have instructional goals. Academic libraries' goals involve teaching their students to do the research they need to complete their course work. Public libraries' instructional goals—although they might not be stated as such—include teaching their patrons to be savvy information consumers, able to do the research they need for their lives. The only reason for committing scarce library resources to a video project is that it will fulfill one or more of the library's missions more quickly, more efficiently, and more cost effectively than other means.

It is useful to create a written goal statement for the video, even if it is just a few sentences. Many later decisions can be answered by reviewing the goal statement and deciding which option would best fulfill that goal.

An example of a goal statement might be, *Inform the public about our summer learning program. Encourage them to contact their local library for more details.* Another might be, *Create a video that will help patrons log into the library's online databases. This video will answer the four most common questions about logging in: username, password, URL, and technical support.*

Academic libraries may want to frame their purpose statement as a set of learning objectives. An example of learning objectives for the patron login video might read as follows:

• Students will be able to list the URL for logging into the library's online resources.
• Student will be able to identify their username.
• Students will be able to identify their password.
• Student will be able to list at least one resource of technical assistance for logging into the library's resources.

Is a Video the Best Way to Teach This?

Is a video the right format to teach the desired skills? Some things are better taught with static pages, lists of instructions, and screenshots. Other subjects will be better served by the immediacy of videos.

If the purpose of the video is to offer an introduction to the library, to make viewers familiar or comfortable with it, a video is an excellent tool. If the purpose is to introduce people and services connected with the library, a video is an excellent tool. If the purpose is to convey a feeling or give an overview of a process—like searching a database—then a video is an excellent tool (Charnigo, 2009, p. 25).

But if the purpose is to teach a step-by-step process or a concept, this might be better taught through text (Leeder, 2009, p. 2). Complex skills, with many options to consider, where patrons need to follow a list of steps, can probably be taught best with a static page (Meehan and Hyland, 2009, p. 25). The text presentation will allow users to scan the page quickly, determine what they need to know, and continue with their work. They will only need to watch the video until they find the information they need; then they can stop the video, complete the action, and turn the video back on. Teaching a patron to download an e-book is an example of a multistep process that might work better as a text page. Teaching students to evaluate the reliability of a journal article they want to use in a research paper is an example of a complicated concept that might work better as a pdf.

Has Anyone Already Created This Video?

Before the library commits time and money to a video project, librarians should do their research to find out if it has already been done. Many database vendors have created videos demonstrating various ways of using their products. It may be most cost effective to link to their video. These can often be found by visiting the vendor website and looking for links titled "training materials," or by searching YouTube.

If the video involves teaching an information literacy concept, there are numerous sources of useful videos on the web. Online repositories of library skills videos include the following:

PRIMO (Peer-Reviewed Instructional Materials Online Database). Offers "instructional materials created by librarians to teach people about discovering, accessing and evaluating information in networked environments." It offers such topics as "Being digital" (tips on thriving in an online environment by managing your online identity, effective searching, and more), how to do a literature review, and much more. http://www.ala.org/cfapps/primo/public/search2.cfm.

Merlot (Multimedia Educational Resource for Learning and Online Teaching). Contains over forty-five thousand "learning objects" on educational topics including information literacy. http://www.merlot.org/.

COIL (Cooperative Online Information Literacy). Project tutorials created by Washington State Community College librarians and published in 2013. Includes such subjects as "Is My Source Credible?" "Generating Keywords and Search Terms," "Recognizing Bias in Information Sources," "Reading Textbooks," and more. http://lstahighlights.wordpress.com/.

What Will It Cost?

Even if the library administration doesn't require it, it is useful to put together a budget for the proposed video. This allows an estimation of the cost of the project and is also helpful in the project's planning stages. If the script calls for a pirate's costume, it is helpful to have obtained one before it is needed on set. Line items in a budget might include the following:

- cost of the planners' and producers' time;
- cost of renting any necessary equipment;
- cost of obtaining editing software;

- payments to actors, narrators, or others;
- cost of any necessary outside technical assistance;
- cost of props or costumes; and
- video hosting charge.

What Are the Organization's Administrative Requirements?

This varies by the scope of the project. A less-than-a-minute screen-capture video on searching a database will typically require few administrative formalities. Larger, more complicated, more costly productions will require more paperwork. This might include script review, inserting institution-approved graphics or branding, obtaining photo or filming releases from anyone who appears in the video, filming permission, and more.

Where Will the Video Be Stored?

Video files need to be stored somewhere. It helps to decide where the new video will be stored early in the planning process, because this could affect decisions about the length of the video, the script, and the equipment and software needed to create the video.

The most common places videos are housed are on the institution's or library's servers, on a free video-storage site such as YouTube, iTunes U, or a paid site like Vimeo. Each of these sites offers pros and cons. Before a decision is made to store the video on any one site, it is best to explore what they offer and what their requirements are.

Library servers may be the easiest place to store the video, but some institutions have little extra server space, or stringent requirements for what can be stored there. Does the department or organization that maintains the institutional servers have file-size or file-format requirements that need to be considered? Do they allow supplementary materials like transcripts to be posted with the videos?

Another option is to host the video on a commercial site such as YouTube or TeacherTube. Commercial sites have several advantages. YouTube, for example, is a robust platform with many backups and redundancies. It is rarely down or inaccessible. Patrons are familiar with it and comfortable with using it (Purcell, 2013). The library can even create its own video channel and put all of its videos together so that patrons can browse them.

This open access, however, does come with some problems. If the video is loaded onto a free commercial site, advertisements could be appended to it (Meehan and Hyland, 2009, p. 26). Usually video creators will not have a voice in whose advertisement is placed with their video, or what the product is. This may be a policy problem for some schools.

Commercial sites may allow users to comment on a video. They typically get more traffic than school server sites, and some of this traffic will be from nonpatrons. Is it acceptable to allow mischievous or hostile viewers to comment? The comment feature can be turned off, but what if viewer comments are desirable? Sometimes patrons' comments can help other users with issues unforeseen by the video creators. The library will probably not wish to commit the resources to monitor the comments regularly. This should be decided before the video is uploaded.

Finally, the visual quality of the video could suffer on commercial sites. The file may be degraded to allow speedy downloading. If, to be effective, the video requires an absolutely clear view of each aspect of the video, a commercial site can pose problems. Video hosting sites like Vimeo, which charge to host videos, will allow the library to avoid unwanted advertising and might solve the quality problem. The yearly charge to maintain this service should be considered and figured into the video budget.

What Kind of Library Resources Are Available?

Make a list of the resources the production team can call upon. The more resources that are found in-house, the fewer will have to be borrowed or rented. Possible resources might include the following:

- Video and editing equipment. Does the library have a store of video equipment? Make an inventory of the available equipment (Johnson, 2010, p. 151). Does the library have a maker-space with video-editing software? Some large libraries have a facility offering video-production and editing services. Take advantage of this (Bolorizadeh et al., 2012, p. 375).
- Does the library have screen-capture software like Camtasia or Captivate, if the video involves screenshots or online work? This can be loaded on the computer, but there are also online sites, including TechSmith and Screencast-O-Matic, that offer both premium and free screen-capture services.
- Library staff. Is there anyone in the library—including librarians or other staff members, student workers, or interns—with video-production experience? Involve them in the process. CSU Northridge's one-minute videos aimed at faculty used the services of classified staff members with experience or education in video production (Martin, 2012, p. 594). Does the library have a Friends of the Library group that can offer some professional assistance?

What external resources are available?

Equipment

Can the library get access to cameras, microphones, lights, and tripods through other school or administrative departments? Does the institution have a video-creating program, either a stand-alone one or through an arts curriculum? If a public library, is there a local government Public Information Office that might be able to lend equipment or expertise? Brainstorm about who might be willing to offer assistance.

Grants

Grants can be used to fund release time for librarians, equipment rentals, and stipends for actors. Look for grants that encourage marketing education services, innovation in teaching, or if working with another academic department, interdisciplinary education.

Free Software

Free screencasting and editing software is available on the web. As of this writing, TechSmith offers Jing, a free, downloadable screencasting software that will let the user make screen-capture videos up to five minutes long (http://www.techsmith.com/jing.html). They can then be uploaded to the web. TechSmith also offers discount prices on other screen-capture software.

Screencast-o-Matic (http://screencast-o-matic.com/) offers web-based screen-capture software. The free version doesn't need to be downloaded onto a library computer. An inexpensive professional version, with useful editing tools, is also available.

Windows Movie Maker is a free basic video-editing software that can be downloaded at http://windows.microsoft.com/. It allows importing of multiple files, basic sound-track editing, and transitions from scene to scene. YouTube also offers some basic editing options.

Do a quick web search to see if new editing or screen-capture services have appeared. As more people make and upload movies, there will be more demand for good editing tools.

Partners

Some academic library videos are the result of library-student collaborations. An advantage of these collaborations is that partners often have training or experience in technical issues such as video lighting and sound quality. Partners have included English, video-production, and business classes (Bisko and Pope-Ruark, 2010, p. 468; Dunne, 2012, p. 37).

Two librarians at York University in Toronto, Canada, worked with their freshman class, creating videos showing new students talking about their experiences developing research and critical-thinking skills (Majekodunmi and Murnaghan, 2012, p. 3). These unscripted videos featured the students being interviewed on such topics as their experience doing research, what they had learned about research after several months in school, and what tips they would give other students about research. At the end of a year, these videos were edited to support the project's learning objectives. The lessons learned included the fact that there were many ways of doing research and that research was recursive—one round of research was often not enough to understand a topic (Majekodunmi and Murnaghan, 2012, p. 7). The response of other students was positive.

At Dublin City University in Ireland, librarians collaborated with students from their School of Communications. They created a suggested script for a library orientation, which the students edited to include their experiences. The students found the equipment, recruited a narrator, and filmed the three-minute video. This was the first of several successful collaborations. The library got high-quality videos, and the students got professional experience and demonstration projects for their portfolios (Dunne, 2012, p. 38).

At Belk Library at North Carolina's Elon University, librarians worked with CUPID (the Center for Undergraduate Publishing and Information Design) to create short videos on library resources (Bisko and Pope-Ruark, 2010, p. 468). The undergraduates interviewed the librarians and then identified the topics they thought would be most interesting to other students. They conducted research, including polls, a survey, a one-question e-mail survey sent to instructors, and reference desk observations. From this they created eight videos on such subjects including accessing databases, printing, and navigating the library. These are now housed on the library website (Bisko and Pope-Ruark, 2010, p. 469).

For public libraries, possible collaborators might include the Friends of the Library group. The members of those groups might have useful skills or resources to help create the video. This could be the kind of exciting project to energize a torpid user group.

PRODUCING THE VIDEO

Whether it is a full-fledged live-action introduction to the library or a quick screen-capture example of searching a local database, there are common steps in producing a video.

Creating a Script

Writing a script—even if it is only descriptions of a series of screenshots—will ensure that everything necessary is covered. A video tells a story, and rereading the script will show whether the story is complete. When writing a script, consider that basic teaching technique "tell them what you intend to teach them, teach them, and restate what you taught them" (Leeder, 2009, p. 2).

Learning objectives determine what is being taught, but there are other decisions that need to be made. What voice should be used to tell this story? When the library or library services are being introduced, a library user voice might appeal to patrons. Humor is good—it catches their attention. When a voice of authority is required, a library staff member might be a better choice.

Shorter is always better from the patron's point of view. They watch these videos to learn something, and that something is often a very specific piece of information. Patrons are less likely to finish longer videos (Henrich and Prorak, 2010, p. 669). Shorter videos are also better for the library. A production made up of short modules is easier to update. When, for example, a vendor updates a user interface, the modules that show this database can be edited while the other modules are left unchanged (Henrich and Attebury, 2012, p. 176).

Have the script reviewed. The best practice would be to have members of the audience for which the script is intended review it. If it is meant for parents, have a group of parents read it. If it is meant for first-year students, have a group of first-year students read it. Their comments will reveal if the script works or not, and they can be a source of helpful suggestions.

Include time to obtain whatever script approval the library or institution's administration requires. Shorter videos, like screen-capture tutorials, will generally require fewer steps in the approval process than longer, live-action videos. In most institutions, projects that require few resources will always be approved faster.

Now consider what the video should be showing. Create a storyboard, a set of graphics that display what each scene of the script should show. This doesn't need to be complex; stick figures will do. It simply needs to be enough to visualize what the final video will look like.

Consider what features will make the video as accessible to hearing- or sight-impaired populations. This could include decisions on font sizes and the colors used in the video. It could also include adding arrows or boxes to highlight content (Oud, 2011, p. 139).

This is a good time to start researching shooting locations. If filming actual locations in the library, consider what the viewer should see—shots of patrons walking, studying, or using the reference desk? What time of day would be best for these shots? Talk to the administration to find out what permissions are needed to film in each script location. Go to the actual location and check out the light. Is it sufficient to shoot a video? (Johnson, 2010, p. 151). If not, plan on getting extra lighting, or on filming elsewhere.

Creating a Production Schedule

For larger video productions, especially those involving a live cast, a production schedule is a valuable tool. A production schedule is a list of what will be required and when. It might be done in a list or spreadsheet form and list the date and time of the shoot, the location, the cast, the crew, what scenes are to be shot, and what equipment and props are required. This planning aid allows the video creators to make sure that the cast is selected in time to read the script, that the equipment is ready, that the permissions to shot have been obtained, and that everything shows up in the right place at the right time. It often helps to break the script down into a list of shots, with notes about what is being said or heard during each shot. This list should describe what the video is showing and will make sure that nothing important has been forgotten (Leeder, 2009, p. 3).

Casting the Video

Many library videos include actual librarians, so patrons will recognize the faces they see at the reference desk (Dabney, 2013, p. 7). Check to see if institutional policies allow the participation of patrons or employees. Many academic libraries have used students or student workers (Majekodunmi and Murnaghan, 2012, p. 3; Martin, 2012, p. 594). Consider doing a casting call, or working with a class or theatrical group on campus. Some patrons might be willing to do this for the experience and the chance to add something to their professional portfolios. Can the library afford to pay video participants? York University gave its student interviewees $10 gift cards (Majekodunmi and Murnaghan, 2012, p. 5).

Gather Equipment and Software

For live-action videos, equipment may include a camera, a lighting source, a good microphone, reflectors, and a tripod (Dabney, 2013, p. 7). Make sure the camera creates a file that the editing software can access, or that the files can be easily converted (Murray, Westwood, and Halford, 2011, p. 47). Green screens, which allow images to be placed behind the actors, can also be helpful (Martin, 2012, p. 595). Costumes and props should be acquired well ahead of the proposed shooting date. One library's polar bear costume was held up in customs, which could have been problematic if it had not been released in time (Thornton and Kaya, 2013, p. 78).

Screen-capture videos require a quiet computer workstation, a good microphone, and screen-capture software. Camtasia, Adobe Captivate, and Snapz Pro are good, inexpensive screen-capture software packages (Tewell, 2010, p. 59). All three include options that make their files accessible (Oud, 2011, p. 130).

Recording the Video

Screen-capture videos have advantages during the creation process. Videos created entirely on the computer can usually be done over a long period of time. They can be worked on one scene at a time, over a period of months. They are also generally shorter and take less time to edit. Expect to make several recording attempts (Mansfield, 2010, p. 17; Meehan and Hyland, 2009, p. 25). These can be cut and edited together to make a satisfying final product.

Live-action videos are going to require at least one period of time when all of the necessary elements—actors, costumes, props, equipment, and lighting—are available. This may be several periods of time, if the filming involves several locations. Bring the storyboards and production schedule to the shooting location. Make sure that everything and everyone listed is present. When filming, consider doing multiple takes so that they can be mixed to give the best result (Gravett and Gill, 2010, p. 68).

During filming, be aware of the light. Are there shadows across the actors' faces? Move, or put the reflectors or extra lighting to use. Be aware of background sound. Consider doing several recordings of any dialogue.

EDITING AND ACCESSIBILITY

Video-editing software will also be required. Two packages that are frequently mentioned in the literature are Final Cut Pro and iMovie (Bolorizadeh et al., 2012, p. 378; Dunne, 2012, p. 39). Windows Movie Maker is free but offers fewer editing options. Audacity is useful for audio editing (Bowles-Terry, Hensley, and Hinchliffe, 2010, p. 18). All of these packages have extensive tutorials, made by both the developers and other users.

As the video is edited, make sure that the final product is as accessible as possible. This includes ensuring that most important commands can be given by keyboard as well as by mouse. It also includes enabling viewers to start and stop the video as needed. Include voice narration that duplicates the information in the graphics (Oud, 2011, p. 134). The narration should be slow paced and clear (Bowles-Terry, Hensley, and Hinchliffe, 2010, p. 23; Mansfield, 2010, p. 17). This will be especially useful for English-as-a-second-language (ESL) students. Include captions and a transcript. Many people without disabilities will appreciate and use the transcripts (Pressley, 2008, p. 20). Save the videos using the latest version of the chosen file format. As newer versions of software come out, more accessibility options become available.

When the video is finished, it is time to test it with people from the target audience. Evaluation can be a formal or informal process.

An informal evaluation might include showing the video to a group of library assistants. Make careful notes about what they have to say. Is there something that should be changed to make the content clearer? Should something be added to make the experience more engaging? Does the video work in all of the venues patrons will try to use it? Do extensive accessibility testing to make sure all users can use the video (Gravett and Gill, 2010, p. 69).

CSU Northridge librarians did a more formal evaluation. They attached a survey to their videos. They asked ten questions, including whether the viewer enjoyed the video, if they learned something new, and what could be done to improve the video (Martin, 2012, p. 597).

MARKETING THE VIDEO

Marketing a new video involves deciding where it should be listed on the library website and then making patrons aware of this new resource.

Linking to the Video

Links should be placed where the patrons will be looking for the information (Bowles-Terry, Hensley, and Hinchliffe, 2010, p. 25). If the video is on logging into the databases, a link should be placed on the database page. If the library has a central page where it lists all its learning resources, the new video should be listed there too. Does the library have all its important information on one gateway page? If the video is on how to access all of the resources behind this gateway page, the video should probably be listed there.

It should be clear what the link offers. "Get Help" is an example of a link that has been found to work (Bowles-Terry, Hensley, and Hinchliffe, 2010, p. 25). After deciding where to place links for the video, the next decision involves advertising it.

Advertising the Video

The advertising campaign for the video depends on what kind of video it is. If it is a major production, then consider a major rollout. Promote it at the reference desk, in the library brochures and other promotional literature, and in library orientations (Gravett and Gill, 2010, p. 70). Put articles in the campus or local newspaper. Post announcements on the library website and the campus blog. Post fliers around the library. Have a world premiere, scheduled for a time when many patrons can attend. Offer snack food and drinks to lure patrons in for a live showing. Mention it in the library's social media. Feature it in Facebook or Twitter. Elon University's Belk Library even had a contest, asking students to create their own videos to promote the library's new collection of instructional videos (Bisko and Pope-Ruark, 2010, p. 470).

A smaller production may merit less publicity but still deserves some attention. If the new video is a screen-capture introduction to a new database, mention it in the library blog, research guides, or subject pathfinders.

Academic librarians should mention pertinent videos in the library orientations and classes that they teach. They may want to ask the instructor to assign them to patrons before the librarian teaches, so that the patrons have some preliminary exposure to the material.

It is also useful to market videos to faculty. A librarian might visit a department meeting, giving a brief presentation highlighting the video. Or she or he could e-mail the department, reminding faculty members they can link to it from inside their classes in the school's Learning Management system. If they have an assignment that uses a particular database, their students will appreciate a link to the tutorial in their online syllabus.

New faculty members might not think of the library when they arrive on campus and start learning about the resources available to them. If your institution has a new faculty orientation, ask to be put on the list of presenters and give the new faculty a list of the available videos, along with the usual promotional materials. If this isn't possible, the institution's human resources department might be willing to give the library a list of new faculty e-mail addresses. A targeted e-mail, giving the faculty a list of video links and pdfs of handouts, could be useful and appreciated.

Try It!

Videos can be thirty-second screencast tutorials on logging into a database, or four-minute live-action introductions to the library, its services, and its resources. They can take as little as ten minutes to create, or as long as a year. They let librarians reach populations that will never come to the reference desk, or even the library. They allow librarians to collaborate with patrons, students, and faculty members to create brief, helpful messages for other faculty members, students, or patrons. A good video is helpful for the viewer and worthwhile for the librarians who learn interesting, eclectic, and valuable new skills. A good video is a win-win proposition.

Finally, a "good video" is not necessarily a flawless video. "Good enough" will do. In-person presentations are never perfect; there is no reason that videos should be (Meehan and Hyland, 2009, p. 25; Schnall, Jankowski, and St. Anna, 2005, p. 80). Patrons know that libraries are not Hollywood studios. They will not expect a multimillion-dollar production. But they will appreciate the library's attempt to meet them where they are: in the video section.

REFERENCES

Bisko, Lynne, and Rebecca Pope-Ruark. (2010). "Makin the Video." *College and Research Libraries News* 71:468–83.

Bolorizadeh, Allison, Michelle Brannen, Rabia Gibbs, and Thura Mack. (2012). "Making Instruction Mobile." *Reference Librarian* 53:373–83.

Bowles-Terry, Melissa, Merinda Kaye Hensley, and Lisa Janicke Hinchliffe. (2010). "Best Practices for Online Video Tutorials in Academic Libraries: A Study of Student Preferences and Understanding." *Communications in Information Literacy* 4:17–28.

Buczynski, James A. (2009). "Bridging the Gap: Video Clip Reference: The Medium Is the Message." *Internet Reference Services Quarterly* 14:37–43.

Charnigo, Laurie. (2009). "Lights! Camera! Action! Producing Library Instruction Videos Using Camtasia Studio." *Journal of Library and Information Services in Distance Learning* 3:23–30.

Dabney, L. Cindy. (2013). "The Art of Making Law Library Videos: Some Tips for Using Videos to Market Your Law Library." *AAL Spectrum* 17:7–8.

Dunne, Siobhán. (2012). "Quid Pro Quo: Harnessing Multimedia Students' Skills to Produce Library Videos." *SCONUL Focus* 56:37–40.

Enis, Matt. (2012). "New LJ Report Closely Examines What Makes Academic Library Patrons Tick." November 5, 2012, Library Journal. http://lj.libraryjournal.com/ (retrieved July 1, 2014).

Gravett, Karen, and Claire Gill. (2010). "Using Online Video to Promote Database Searching Skills: The Creation of a Virtual Tutorial for Health and Social Care Students." *Journal of Information Literacy* 4:66–71.

Henrich, Kristin J., and Ramirose I. Attebury. (2012). "Using Blackboard to Assess Course-Specific Asynchronous Library Instruction." *Internet Reference Services Quarterly* 17:167–79.

Henrich, Kristin J., and Diane Prorak. (2010). "A School Mascot Walks into the Library: Tapping School Spirit for Library Instruction Videos." *Reference Services Review* 38:663–75.

Johnson, Wendell G. (2010). "Instructional Video for the Community College Library." *Community and Junior College Libraries* 16:151–52.

Leeder, Kim. (2009). "Learning to Teach through Video." *In the Library with the Lead Pipe* (October): 1–6.

Majekodunmi, Norda, and Kent Murnaghan. (2012). "'In Our Own Words': Creating Videos and Teaching and Learning Tools." *Partnership: Canadian Journal of Library and Information Practice and Research* 7:1–12.

Mansfield, Daren. (2010). "No Audition Required! Using Video Tutorials in the 24x7 Age." *SCONUL Focus* 49:16–18.

Martin, Coleen Meyers. (2012). "One-Minute Video: Marketing Your Library to Faculty." *Reference Services Review* 40:589–600.

Meehan, David, and Jack Hyland. (2009). "Video Killed the 'PDF' Star: Taking Information Resources Guides Online." *SCONUL Focus* 47:23–26.

Murray, Liz, Helen Westwood, and Samantha Halford. (2011). "Veni, Vidi, Video . . . Making a Library Video for New Students." *SCONUL Focus* 54:45–49.

National Center for Education Statistics. (2014). "Characteristics of Postsecondary Faculty." Condition of Education. http://nces.ed.gov/.

Oud, Joanne. (2011). Improving Screencast Accessibility for People with Disabilities: Guidelines and Techniques." *Internet Reference Services Quarterly* 16:129–44.

Pressley, Lauren. (2008). "Using Videos to Reach Site Visitors: A Toolkit for Today's Student." *Computers in Libraries* 28:18–22.

Purcell, Kristen. (2013). "Online Video 2013." Pew Internet Research Project. http://www.pewinternet.org (retrieved June 24, 2014).

Schnall, Janet G., Terry Ann Jankowski, and Leilani A. St. Anna. (2005). "Using Camtasia to Enhance Web Instruction Pages and Tutorials." *Journal of Hospital Librarianship* 5:80.

Tewell, Eamon. (2010). "Video Tutorials in Academic Art Libraries: A Content Analysis and Review." *Art Documentation* 29:53–61.

Thornton, David E., and Ebru Kaya. (2013). "All the World Wide Web's a Stage: Improving Students Information Skills with Dramatic Video Tutorials." *ASLIB Proceedings: New Information Perspectives* 66:73–87.

Zickuhr, Kathryn, Kristen Purcell, and Lee Rainie. (2014). "From Distant Admirers to Library Lovers—and Beyond." http://www.pewinternet.org/.

Chapter Five

Using Research-Based Guidelines for Developing Mobile Information Technologies

A Literature Review and Recommendations

Dawn Paschal, Donald E. Zimmerman, and Teresa Yohon

Over the past two decades, academic libraries have faced major challenges with keeping their websites current and usable as budgets withered and web technologies evolved at a dizzying pace. Now new demands are being placed on library website development with the rapid adoption of mobile technologies following Apple's introduction of the iPhone in 2007 and the iPad in 2010.

Mobile technologies include any battery-powered device that enables users to connect to mobile phone services and the Internet wirelessly. In 2014, the more commonly used mobile devices include cell phones, smartphones, tablets, e-readers, and laptops. Users access their mobile phone service and the Internet while moving or stationary. They can read the information interactively while accessing it, or they can access it, download it, and read, listen, or view it later.

Mobile technologies change users' behaviors. Forrester Research, a market research firm, reports that people are experiencing a *mobile mind shift* that is creating *mobile moments* (Schadler, Bernoff, and Ask, 2014, p. 1). They suggest mobile moments occur at a point in time and space, when users pull out a mobile device to seek the information they need.

Library patrons are bringing their behaviors and expectations about mobile technologies to their information seeking in libraries. Libraries need to embrace users' mobile moments too. Consider Forrester's findings as people's expectation of information convenience—that is, finding what they want, when they want it, wherever they are by using mobile technologies.

The rapid rise of mobile technologies and the developing body of academic research on mobile technologies suggests a shift in use of mobile technologies by library patrons. Librarians and libraries need to consider the following:

- What are the major challenges that libraries face in meeting the needs of mobile library users?
- How can libraries ensure the usability of library websites designed for mobile devices?
- How do libraries employ a cost-effective website design strategy?
- How can librarians gain the needed skills to understand and use various mobile technologies, recognize and analyze trends, and respond strategically?

To help librarians answer these questions, this chapter discusses the following:

- The rise of mobile technologies
- Libraries and mobile technologies
- Responsive web design
- Lessons from research and evaluation
- A stepwise, research-based approach for moving to responsive design
- Research needed on mobile technologies
- Strategies for keeping abreast of digital technology adoption and library usage

This chapter was developed in collaboration with programmers and lessons learned from usability testing, as well as reviews of the academic and trade literature included in databases covering library science, communication science, website design, human computer interactions, technology transfer/diffusion of innovation, and usability testing.

THE RISE OF MOBILE TECHNOLOGIES

Clearly, the adoption of mobile technologies (smartphones, tablets, e-readers, and related technologies) and their use to access the Internet is rising and will continue to do so for years. Some mobile technologies have reached near total penetration—adoption by nearly every adult—in selected demographic profiles.

Based on a May 2013 Pew survey of 2,252 adults, age eighteen and older, 70 percent of American adults have broadband connections at home (Pew Research Center, 2014, p. 1; Zickuhr and Smith, 2013, p. 1), and in homes above $75,000 annual income, 88 percent have broadband connections. Of these, 46 percent of adult Americans have both home broadband connections and smartphones, and 10 percent have a smartphone but no home broadband connection.

Based on a January 2014 survey of 1,006 U.S. Internet users, 87 percent of the adults connect to the Internet (Fox and Rainie, 2014, p. 1); 99 percent of adults living in households earning $75,000 or more used the Internet; 97 percent of eighteen- to twenty-nine-year-olds did, as did 97 percent of adults with college degrees. Some 53 percent of the respondents reported that it would be "very hard to give up" access to the Internet.

Based on an April–May 2013 Pew national telephone survey of 2,252 adults, eighteen years and older, some 91 percent of adult Americans have a cell phone and 56 percent of all adult Americans use their cell phones to access the Internet (Pew Research Center, 2014; Smith, 2013, pp. 1–5). More specifically, 90 percent of the eighteen- to twenty-nine-year-olds in households above $75,000 own smartphones, as do 87 percent of thirty- to forty-nine-year-olds, 72 percent of fifty- to sixty-four-year-olds, and 43 percent of sixty-five-year-olds and older (Smith, 2013, pp. 1–5).

As of January 2014, 50 percent of American adults own either a tablet or an e-reader (Zickuhr and Rainie, 2014, p. 1); the adoption of mobile technologies continues steadily.

Between October 15 and November 10, 2012, the Pew Research Center's Internet and American Life Project, underwritten by a grant from the Bill and Melinda Gates Foundation, surveyed 2,252 Americans sixteen years and older to assess their views on library services (Zickuhr, Rainie, and Purcell, 2013, p. 4). The researchers found that library patrons were eager to see libraries' digital services expand, while print books will remain important.

When asked about online research services, 37 percent of the respondents reported they would be "very likely" to use such services, and another 36 percent reported they would be "somewhat likely" to use such services. When asked about apps-based access to library materials and services, 35 percent reported they would be "very likely" to use them, and another 28 percent said they would be "somewhat likely" to do so. When asked about GPS navigation apps to find resources in libraries, 34 percent reported they would be "very likely" to use them, and 28 percent reported they would be "somewhat likely" to use them. When asked about using an "Amazon"-style customized book/audio/video recommendation based on their searches, 29 percent reported they would be "very likely" to use it, and another 35 percent said they would be "somewhat likely" to use it.

In the final phase of the Internet and American Life study, the researchers surveyed 6,224 Americans, and from that data set, the researchers created divided profiles of different kinds of library users (Zickuhr, Purcell, and Rainie, 2014). The researchers divided respondents into (1) highly engaged (Library Lovers, 10 percent; Information Omnivores, 20 percent); (2) medium engaged (Solid Center, 30 percent; Print Traditionalists, 9 percent); (3) low engagement (Not for Me, 4 percent; Young and Restless, 7 percent; Rooted and Roadblocked, 7 percent); and (4) no personal use of a library—that is, never used a library (Distant Admirers, 10 percent; Off the Grid, 4 percent).

While the highly engaged library users—that is, Library Lovers and Information Omnivores—generally use the Internet frequently and use cell phones, tablets, or other mobile devices, those classified as Solid Center, Not for Me, and the Young and Restless had similar patterns of the adoption of mobile technologies (see table 5.1).

Clearly, the demand for mobile technologies will continue to grow for years. Anshul Gupta, Gartner, a market analysis company, predicted that the sales of high-end smartphones would slow while the sales of low- and mid-price smartphones are increasing in 2014 (Reuters, 2014). Worldwide, smartphone sales accounted for 53.6 percent of overall sales in 2013. Further, Gupta predicted smartphone sales to increase to 1.2 to 1.3 billion units in 2014.

International Data Corporation predicted that by 2017 the total smartphone shipments worldwide would be about 1.7 billion units, and of these about 189 million units will be shipped in North America (Llamas and Reith, 2013, p. 1). Canalys, another analysis firm, predicted tablets would make up 50 percent of PC sales in 2014, with shipments in 2017 growing to 396 million units (Canalys, 2013, p. 2).

LIBRARIES AND MOBILE TECHNOLOGIES

Academic librarians could not possibly have overlooked the swift proliferation of smartphones and mobile devices since 2007, when Apple introduced the iPhone with its touch-screen interface, and the development of diverse Android smartphones following shortly thereafter. Apple released its first iPad in 2010, and again various competitors released their own versions of the tablet.

A number of studies have yielded a wealth of data on the adoption of mobile technologies. The 2012 *Pearson Foundation Survey on Students and Tablets* summary notes that "tablet ownership has more than tripled among college students since March 2011, with one-quarter of students now owning a standard tablet" (p. 2), while the 2013 *ECAR Study of Undergraduate* survey of 6,224 Americans age sixteen and older conducted July 18–September 30, 2013 (Zickuhr, Purcell, and Rainie, 2014).

Activities	Library Lovers	Information Omnivores	Solid Center	Print Tradition-alists	Not for Me	Young and Rest-less	Rooted and Road-blocked	Distant Admirers	Off the Grid
Internet use & online activities									
Use the Internet at least occasionally	95%	97%	87%	87%	78%	90%	74%	72%	56%
Access the Internet on cell phone, tablet, or other mobile device	72%	81%	69%	63%	62%	82%	51%	54%	45%
Broadband at home	77%	86%	72%	67%	66%	76%	58%	51%	37%
Use the Internet every day or almost every day (among Internet users)	84%	90%	82%	74%	78%	82%	78%	70%	68%
Mobile devices and e-readers									
Have a cell phone (to include smartphones)	92%	95%	91%	91%	89%	93%	84%	88%	77%
Have a smartphone	58%	68%	57%	47%	52%	68%	40%	41%	33%
Have tablet computer	39%	46%	35%	29%	31%	36%	24%	27%	19%
Have an e-reader, like Kindle or Nook	30%	33%	22%	24%	20%	24%	20%	18%	12%

Students and Information Technology reports that 77 percent of undergraduate students said they own a smartphone (Dahlstrom, Walker, and Dziuban,
2013, p. 25).

Another study of interest is the Pew Research Center's *Smartphone Ownership 2013* (Smith, 2013, p. 3); this survey of American adults reveals that
79 percent of those aged eighteen to twenty-four own a smartphone, and 81
percent of adults aged twenty-five to thirty-four. The center's 2014 "E-Reading Rises as Device Ownership Jumps" (Zickuhr and Rainie, 2014, p. 2)
notes that 50 percent of American adults own either a tablet or an e-reader.
More specifically, 42 percent own tablets, and 32 percent own e-readers.
While these Pew studies do not focus solely on the nation's college students,
they do examine mobile device ownership of the current and potential university student population.

Following the rapid speed with which mobile technologies were adopted
across the country, the commercial sector seized the initiative in creating
mobile content; Geoffrey Little (2011, p. 267) noted in 2011 that information
provider partners of academic libraries, including ARTStor, Cambridge Journals Online, Elsevier Health, Gale, IEEE, JSTOR, LexisNexis, Wiley, and
WorldCat, were offering mobile services such as websites and applications
for accessing scholarly journals, images, or databases. Now ProQuest/UMI's
ebrary provides mobile access to a collection of scholarly e-books in a variety of subject areas; ThirdIron's BrowZine organizes and delivers articles to
mobile devices for browsing, reading, and monitoring of scholarly journals in
a newsstand format; and the Overdrive digital media service distributes e-
books, audiobook collections, music, and video to academic and other libraries. Some vendors of library management systems offer mobile catalog solutions, such as the Innovative Interfaces' AirPAC service, a portable version
of its Millennium online public access catalog (OPAC); and SirsiDynix has
PocketCirc, a tool for library staff that enables remote support of circulation-
related activities.

How have academic libraries responded to the dramatic rise of mobile
technologies in American society? Medical librarians were among the first
adopters in the early 2000s, and since about 2009 a growing number of
academic libraries have steadily followed suit. In general, however, academic libraries have been slow to embrace the mobile revolution; a 2010 study,
"Universities and Libraries Move to the Mobile Web," revealed that just 24
of the 111 English-speaking members of the Association of Research Libraries (ARL) had launched separate mobile websites for their universities and
libraries, or for their libraries only (Aldrich, 2010, p. 5). The number of both
ARL and non-ARL libraries with a mobile web presence continues to climb,
and a quick online search currently shows that libraries at Alberta, Ball State,
Boston College, Brigham Young, Colorado State, Cornell, Duke, Indiana,
Maryland, McGill, MIT, Northwestern, North Carolina State, Rice, Rich-

mond, Oregon State, Sam Houston State, Stanford, Utah State, and Virginia are all offering various mobile services and collections. Often these sites provide information on library hours, locations, news and events, maps/directions, services, and exhibits, plus access to research guides, articles and databases, e-journals, and resources such as Google Scholar, Google Books, and the Hathi Trust Digital Library, all specially formatted for smaller screens.

To date, little literature or research has been published on usability or desired features of academic library mobile websites, and what has appeared tends to include the latter. For example, respondents to a 2008 survey conducted by librarians at Ryerson University revealed they were most interested in the ability to check the library catalog and their borrowing records, in finding information on library hours and schedules, and in an option to book group study rooms (Wilson and McCarthy, 2010, p. 216). The California Digital Library, via surveys and interviews, found in 2010 that 55 percent of mobile users were interested in searching the library catalog frequently or occasionally. Respondents (53 percent) were also interested in the option to access databases either frequently or occasionally (Hu and Meier, 2010, p. 27), probably not for actual research purposes, but to retrieve known items or information quickly. In 2011, librarians at Utah State University surveyed students on mobile access and found that 16 percent of respondents wanted access to the library catalog, 11 percent said they wanted mobile services in general, 10 percent desired access to journal articles, and 9 percent expressed interest in the ability to reserve study rooms using a mobile device (Dresselhaus and Shrode, 2012, p. 91).

EXPLORING RESPONSIVE WEB DESIGN

To date, libraries have embraced two strategies for programming their websites: (1) developing multiple stand-alone websites for desktop computers, smartphones, tablets, and other mobile technologies; and, more recently, (2) employing responsive design for websites—an emerging alternative to developing multiple websites.

Ethan Marcotte (2010) proposed the use of responsive design for mobile websites, which enables programmers to develop one website so that users can view all of its content on a wide range of devices—such as desktops, tablets, e-readers, and smartphones. While developing a website using responsive design may be more expensive, it is less costly than building multiple websites for specific mobile devices. Few if any libraries can afford to build dozens of individual websites for each different device that a patron might use to access the library website. Thus, responsive design can be a cost savings overall for libraries.

To illustrate just how complex the mobile environment is currently, the Windows operating systems for personal computers allows landscape (horizontal) resolutions to be set between 1,920 × 1,200 pixels and 800 × 600 pixels with a recommendation of 1,920 × 1,200 pixels for desktop computers. Resolutions vary for mobile technologies and with different models. In late spring 2014, Apple's Air iPad, iPad, and iPad mini had 2,048 × 1,536 pixel resolution at 264 pixels per inch; Samsung's Galaxy Note 10.1, a ten-inch screen, used 2,560 × 1,600 pixel resolution; Apple's iPhone 5s and 5c used 1,136 × 640 pixel resolution, and the iPhone 4s used 960 × 640 resolution; and Samsung Galaxy S5 used 1,920 × 1,080 pixel resolution. Further, mobile technologies allow users to rotate from vertical (portrait) to horizontal (landscape). Undoubtedly, the proliferation of mobile devices using diverse resolutions will continue for some years to come.

The core components of responsive-design programming use a document structure, CSS (cascading style sheets, which minimize coding specific content elements); flexible grids, layouts, and images; and media queries (Hamilton, 2014). Flexible grids and flexible images allow the images and text to fit the screen size of different devices. Media queries are points in the code—that is, break points—that require loading a new set of styles—media type and maximum device width to resize and arrange the content to fit the devices with different screen resolutions (Marcotte, 2010, p. 4; Reidsma, 2014, p. 43). In doing so, the website elements, which are traditionally designed for horizontal presentation, will be rearranged into a vertical arrangement.

Originally, programmers used fixed pixel widths for coding website and website components. In contrast, responsive design requires programming using fluid layouts. Rather than coding fixed pixel widths, programmers code websites using flexible design—that is, percentages of screen widths and depths.

Discussions explaining library use of responsive design are just beginning to be reported in the scholarly literature. Robert Fox (2012, p. 119) argues for libraries to adopt responsive design and stressed that doing so would put those libraries ahead of the curve as more and more patrons adopt the growing number of mobile devices for accessing the Internet. Bohyun Kim (2013, p. 29) defines and illustrates responsive design, explains and provides responsive-design examples, and discusses its potential pitfalls.

Before redesigning Oregon State University's mobile website, librarians Hannah Rempel and Laurie Bridges (2013, p. 8) surveyed patrons (n = 115) and analyzed web analytics of their library's website usage. They then explained why they turned to responsive design (p. 20) for the full website and the mobile website (p. 21). The library's programmer developed the Oregon State University's website using Drupal (https://www.drupal.org/), an open-source, content-data-management system.

Lisa Gayhart, Bilal Khalid, and Gordon Belray (2014, pp. 1–17) provide and illustrate a case study of the University of Toronto's library development of a new catalog using responsive design. They report that the responsive-design website provided a mobile-friendly, flexible, and intuitive library catalog without compromising its quality or performance.

Frank Cervone (2013, pp. 130–33) reports that libraries can use responsive design to enhance accessibility of digital library collections by patrons with disabilities.

In the first chapter of *Responsive Web Design for Libraries*, published by the American Library Association, Matthew Reidsma (2014, pp. 1–15) argues that libraries use responsive design and follows with an overview of its composition and programming. Throughout the remaining eight chapters, Reidsma provides additional points supporting responsive design while demonstrating specifics for coding responsive design.

LESSONS FROM RESEARCH AND EVALUATION

As of summer 2014, empirical research articles exploring mobile technology interface design are just beginning to appear in the academic literature. Few articles report research on interface design for library mobile technologies. Therefore, the following discussion first summarizes the databases reviewed and then provides brief reviews of selected articles applicable to mobile technologies.

Databases reviewed included EBSCO Academic Search Premier, Agricola, Applied Science and Technology Abstracts, Biological Abstracts, Business Source Complete, Business Source Premier, Communication and Mass Media Complete, ERIC, Library Literature and Information Science Index, PsycINFO, Web of Science, and Library, Information Science and Technology Abstracts.

Jakob Nielsen, a well-known web guru, began arguing in his column (http://www.useit.com/) for fast download times in the 1990s, and he continues to do so based on multiple usability evaluations. A ten-second delay will often make users leave a website immediately (Nielsen, 2010, p. 2).

No academic journal articles reporting research or evaluations of the impact of download speeds for library websites were found. That said, searches of the Internet identified columns reporting findings of user studies of business websites. For example, Akamai Technologies, Inc. (2010, p. 1) reported that 57 percent of shoppers will wait three seconds before abandoning sites providing travel information and that eighteen- to twenty-four-year-olds expect a site to load in two seconds or less.

Download speeds of websites depend on a variety of factors. For desktop computers, the website size, hardwired broadband connection speed, RAM, processor speed, and other factors influence download speed. For mobile technologies, additional factors determine download speed. Tammy Everts (2013, pp. 53, 54) identified three technical limiting factors for mobile technology performance: (1) web pages are bigger than ever, (2) latency can vary widely, (3) and download speeds can produce huge variances. She pointed out that the average web page runs about 1 MB and contains eighty resources, such as images, JavaScript, CSS, and so forth (pp. 53–54). Projections suggest websites could contain more than 2 MB by 2015. Mobile latency—that is, response time—is inconsistent because of weather, location, and other factors (p. 54). She noted that the average U.S. broadband speed is 15 MBsp and that 3G networks can be up to fifteen times slower than broadband, while LTE can be up to twice as fast (p. 54). Everts recommends programming techniques to speed website download times for mobile technologies.

Once downloaded, the website home design page and links determine whether users will further explore the website. David Robins and Jason Holmes (2008, p. 386) explored the correlations between users' perceptions of web page aesthetics and credibility using twenty graduate students from library information sciences. The researchers downloaded twenty-one home pages, saved them on a local computer, and then stripped them of all visual enhancements (p. 391). Participants judged pages with higher aesthetic features to have higher credibility, but the researchers found no significant difference in the time required to assess credibility (p. 394)—and they pointed out that such judgments were made within a few seconds of viewing a page. Likewise, Gitte Lindgaard and colleagues (2006, p. 115) found that visual-appeal ratings were critical and suggested that website designers have about fifty milliseconds to make a good first impression.

Junho Choi and Hye-Jin Lee (2012) hypothesize that the perceived simplicity of smartphone interfaces influences positive user satisfaction (p. 133). To assess the hypothesis, the researchers sent text messages to four hundred people attending a large university in Seoul, South Korea, and asked them to complete an online questionnaire. Of the 205 smartphone users who responded, 52 percent used an iPhone and 48 percent used other smartphones. Using structural equation modeling, the researchers reported that their findings imply that simplified interface design contributed significantly to the positive evaluation of users' interactions with their smartphones.

One technique that may enhance users' experiences is rotating mobile technologies in the landscape view. Christopher Sanchez and Russell Branaghan (2011, p. 793) compared user reasoning when using small devices in the portrait and landscape orientations. Turning small-screen devices to the landscape orientation improved performance, and the landscape orientation appeared to provide more support for individuals with lower-working (short-term) memory capacity.

Legibility of text and icons on websites and mobile technologies remains critical to all websites. Daisuke Saito, Keiichi Saito, and Masao Saito (2010) assessed the contrast levels between text and background when websites are displayed on desktop computers. They found that reading time increased when the contrast decreased—that is, font/background colors (Saito, Saito, and Saito, 2010, p. 27). They use the highest average reading time at the highest commonly used contrast (92.5 percent) as a reference to normalize the data (Saito, Saito, and Saito, 2010, p. 30). When they found a positive correlation—that is, highest contrast of text to background—the spread between participants was small, but under negative correlation—low contrast of text to background—the difference between participants was large (p. 31).

Barbara Chaparro and colleagues (2010, p. 36) compared on-screen legibility of six ClearType fonts and two widely used regular fonts. They found that legibility was higher for ClearType Consolas and Cambria fonts as well as non-ClearType Verdana fonts, when compared to Times New Roman.

Studying the use of simulated Simens S45 cell phones on desktop computers by participants forty years and older, Martina Ziefle (2010, p. 719) found navigation performance was optimal when twelve-point (letter size 4 mm) font size was presented, and the lowest performance was with eight-point (letter size 2.5 mm) type. Further, Ziefle found navigation performance was optimal when the font size and preview were large.

Preethy Pappachan and Ziefle (2008) investigated possible cultural differences in comprehending icons used on mobile technologies. They found no difference in comprehension of users across cultures; the more detailed the icons and more concrete the icons, the more correctly they were interpreted (p. 331).

Chrysoula Gatsou, Anastasios Politis, and Dimitrios Zevgolis (2011) compare novices, by age group, in their navigation using either text or icons. They found that younger users preferred visual—that is, icons—while older users preferred text buttons.

Earlier research on websites displayed on-screen suggested that breadth website structure was preferred to depth website structures. Avi Parush and Nirit Yuviler-Gavish (2004, p. 753) found that navigation performance was better on the broad navigation structure compared to the hierarchy structure on cell phones.

Based on an extensive review of color and its role on websites, Terri Holtze (2006, pp. 98–99) recommended the following strategies for using color on them:

- Never use color alone to indicate an important feature.
- Limit the use of fully saturated colors to reduce eye strain.
- Maximize readability by using sufficient luminescence to increase contrast between text and background colors.

- Consider setting the background to a soothing color on slow-loading pages.
- Reduce distraction by eliminating graphics behind text.
- Consider age and culture of your audience when choosing colors.
- Follow standards (e.g., blue hyperlinks), and use color consistently.
- Do not place red and green next to each other because they are indistinguishable for people with the more common form of color-deficiency vision.
- Avoid placing red and blue (spectrally opposite) colors adjacent to one another, as they may appear blurry.
- Test the colors: on different people, on different devices, and for how they will appear to people with color-deficient vision.

While Joanna Lumsden's (2008) monograph addresses usability problems and the challenges of mobile technologies with smaller interfaces, it still provides valuable insights to designing and evaluating the ever-changing mobile technologies. In the two-volume monograph, Lumsden provides sixty-four chapters written by researchers with diverse mobile technology expertise. Section 1 provides twenty-three chapters focusing on interface design; section 2 provides twelve chapters on novel interaction techniques; section 3 provides seven chapters on assistive technologies; section 4 provides seventeen chapters on evaluation techniques; and section 5 provides five case studies. Of special note, section 1 on interface and design topics covers ethnography, photo management, transgenerational design features, design individuals with disabilities, wearable computers, context of mobile technology use, in-car interfaces, speech-based user interfaces, museums, designs for learning, intelligent interfaces, and rapid prototyping mobile designs.

Anne Mangen, Bente Walgermo, and Kolbjørn Brønnick (2013, p. 61) compare seventy-two Norwegian tenth graders' reading comprehension for reading 1,400- to 2,000-word texts in either a print (hard copy) or a pdf copy on a PC screen. The researchers found that students reading the print versions scored significantly higher on comprehension scores than did students reading the pdf file online.

A STEPWISE, RESEARCH-BASED APPROACH FOR MOVING TO RESPONSIVE DESIGN

As with any project, creating a mobile library website requires thoughtful planning. Chad Mairn (2013, p. 86) recommends first studying use of the complete website to determine those parts of the full website to include in the mobile-optimized version. Then determine who will design it and decide which resources and services to include; consider that every feature on the full website may not function on a mobile version, mainly because third-party browser plug-ins are not compatible with the majority of mobile browsers (Mairn, 2013, p. 86). It is also important to ask users what they desire in a mobile experience. Keep in mind that changing a website abruptly can cause problems for users; Reidsma (2014, p. 63) suggests changing an existing website incrementally over time to avoid confusing them.

Consider a top-down approach—that is, design the website for a desktop computer using fluid designs and then program it for mobile technologies, ensuring the site provides the content desired (see appendix 1). For a detailed approach on programming, see Lynda.com's more than twenty responsive-design courses and over seven hundred responsive-design videos.

A caution about responsive design: responsive design—like all website design, development, and programming—is not without pitfalls. Kim (2013, p. 32) cautions that poorly designed websites using responsive design can be just as cumbersome as websites created without responsive design. Clutter can produce poor responsive-design websites with limited usability. While focusing on business applications, Jeremy Durant (2014) provides five reasons responsive design can fail; of those five, four are most applicable to library responsive-design websites: lengthy copy, unappealing images, long videos, and unfriendly navigation. Cautious librarians considering responsive design should first brief themselves and their programmers through reviews of the growing resources on responsive design, including trade books and tutorials, such as those that http://www.lynda.com/ provides.

RESEARCH NEEDED ON MOBILE TECHNOLOGIES

Based on the foregoing discussion, librarians face four major challenges: (1) changing mobile technologies, (2) changing website programing, (3) changing expectations of library users, and (4) changing how patrons interact with library websites displayed on mobile technologies.

Additional research is needed to advise the development of guidelines for website developers—programmers and content developers—so they can create better library websites. Additional research is also needed for mobile technology interface design; based on Zimmerman and Yohon's (2007) recommendations in this area, we have some suggestions (see appendix 2).

LOOKING FORWARD

As technologies changed over the last fifty years, libraries and the publishing industry have steadily moved from paper-based formats to digital. No doubt technologies will continue to change, requiring libraries to adapt ever-expanding ways patrons will access and use them.

How then will libraries keep pace with continuously evolving technologies to better serve their patrons? The following discussion provides an overview of strategies to help librarians

- keep abreast of patrons' digital technology adoption and library use;
- explore responsive web design as it evolves; and
- identify research-based recommendations for website design.

Keeping Abreast of Digital Technology Adoption and Library Usage

Consider the annual reports of the Pew Foundation's Internet and American Life Project. Using nationwide random phone surveys, online surveys, and qualitative research, the center investigates Americans' use of the Internet and its influences on their lives (Pew Research Center, 2014) and predicts Internet usage through 2025 (Anderson and Rainie, 2014). Of special note is the center's "From Distant Admirers to Library Lovers—and Beyond" (Zickuhr, Purcell, and Rainie, 2014). While the researchers created a typology of library users and document their differences in technology use (see table 5.1), the researchers found that printed books remain central to America's library use and only 4 percent of Americans read only e-books (Zickuhr, Purcell, and Rainie, 2014, p. 8).

While the Pew Foundation provides a national picture of Americans' adoption of digital technologies, Internet use, library usage, and reading practices, libraries can benefit greatly from researching the needs, preferences, and expectations of their local patrons.

In *User Studies for Digital Library Development*, Milena Dobreva, Andy O'Dwyer, and Pierluigi Feliciati (2012) provide a carefully conceptualized overview of methods used to study patrons, case studies of users, cultural heritage studies, and recommendations for developing and executing studies of library patrons. While Dobreva, O'Dwyer, and Feliciati (2012, p. 7) caution that their monograph is not a research methods handbook, they provide succinct introductions to applicable social science research methodologies and brief case studies illustrating digital library topics.

In *The Handheld Library: Mobile Technology and the Librarian*, editors Thomas Peters and Lori Bell (2013) compiled nineteen chapters exploring mobile technology trends and libraries, mobile library users, access to content, mobile references, and mobile professional development opportunities. Each chapter provides detailed guidance and insights on the respective topics.

While an in-depth discussion of social science methodologies is beyond the scope of this chapter, we have gained useful lessons about library users and faculty members by conducting focus groups, nominal group technique sessions, print and online surveys, and usability testing. Social science research methodologies are fraught with pitfalls for the unwary. Studying social science research methods handbooks and collaborating with empirical social scientists can help librarians minimize social science pitfalls. The following resources provide useful guidance.

Dillman, D. A. (2007). *Mail and Internet surveys*. Hoboken, NJ: Wiley.
Krueger, R. A. (2014). *Focus groups: A practical guide for applied research*. 5th ed. Thousand Oaks, CA: Sage.
Rossi, P. H., Lipsey, M. W., and Freeman, H. E. (2004). *Evaluation: A systematic approach*. 7th ed. Thousand Oaks, CA: Sage.
U.S. Department of Health and Human Services. (2014). *Usability.gov: Improving the user experience*. Retrieved June 5, 2014, from http://www.usability.gov/.

Exploring Responsive Web Design Development

For guidance on website coding standards, accessibility, and related topics for the World Wide Web, the World Wide Web Consortium (http://www.w3.org/) website provides useful information; it explains and documents the coding standards, updates for coding websites, and website statistics.

In addition, one can consult the W3 Schools (http://www.w3schools.com/) for easy-to-use site lessons on HTML, Java scripts, XML, and server side coding. Lynda.com provides more than five hundred courses on website development.

Identifying Research-Based Recommendations for Website Design

For guidance on research-based website design, librarians can review the U.S. Department of Health and Human Services (HHS) website http://www.usability.gov/. The agency created it in 2003, and HHS expanded and updated the website in 2006 and posted a revised website in July 2013. In announcing the new site, Richard Stapleton (2013, p. 1) pointed out, "We note the growing role of UX (user experience) plays in social media and on the mobile platform. We used our re-boot as an opportunity to explore mobile-first design, going beyond responsive design to design for touch and then reverse engineering for the more traditional click and scroll." Stapleton then explained that the agency lab tested the evolving design. They used Drupal to design a smartphone screen for mobile-first model and then expanded the design size to be responsive.

Usability.gov contains outstanding research-based discussions and recommendations on usability testing and remains a must-read for individuals new to usability testing as well as seasoned experts. The site contains clear discussion of usability project management, usability testing methods, templates and documents, guidelines, the how and why of usability, how-to and tools, management recommendations, content strategy, and visual design.

Of special note are the eighteen chapters containing more than two hundred research-based guidelines. Each indicates the document type, topic, guideline, comments, and the sources—that is, the academic journal or conference citation upon which the guideline is based. Further, each guideline is rated on its importance on a one to five scale with five being the most important; additionally, the strength-of-evidence rating has been assigned indicating the level of support by research or expert opinion.

For another perspective on usability for mobile technologies, see *Mobile Usability* (Nielsen and Budiu, 2013). The researchers document and provide guidance for usability testing of regular cell phones (small screens), smartphones (mid-sized screens), and full-screen phones, such as iPhone, Android, and Windows phones.

Lumsden's (2008) seventeen chapters of section 7 are well worth reviewing. They provide more detailed strategies applicable to the ever-evolving mobile technologies. Topics covered include theoretical perspectives, specialized usability evaluation methods, context for usability testing, heuristic usability, usability methodology guidelines, cognitive models, privacy considerations, eye tracking, and laboratory and field usability testing.

Consider exploring Digital Government (https://www.digitalgov.gov/), from the Office of Citizen Services and Innovative Technologies, established by the U.S. General Services Administration. The office supports the digital efforts of federal government agencies and helps build relationships with state and local government agencies providing information to U.S. citizens. It has formed working groups to help package content for delivery by smartphones, tablets, Twitter, Facebook, Instagram, and agency desktop websites. A careful review of this office's website can be useful.

Commercial resources also provide guidance for keeping abreast of advances in digital information delivery. Adobe provides regular reports on advances in digital technology relevant to software development. Crown, a full service e-business firm in conjunction with Adobe, produced Adobe's 2014 white paper "Return on Responsive Web Design." That white paper documented that websites are receiving more traffic from tablets than smartphones and that users view 70 percent more pages per visit when browsing with a tablet compared to smartphones (Adobe, 2014, p. 1). Such findings suggest that smartphones remain more difficult for patrons to use than tablets or desktop devices. Adobe also provides a rationale and cost justification for using responsive design.

AdobeTV (http://tv.adobe.com/) provides dozens of free video tutorials and informational videos on a wide range of Adobe products. Adobe also provides case studies of how different organizations develop mobile apps.

As of summer 2014, Lynda.com, a fee-based online tutorial vendor, provided courses on responsive design. With an annual license, librarians can access more than 2,500 courses—that is, tutorials on digital technologies, creative techniques, business practices, and related topics. Additional tutorials on digital technology and management practices are added weekly. The tutorials, presented by expert instructors on the respective topic, are well done and easy to follow.

CONCLUDING REMARKS

The mobile revolution has been well documented by various studies and is in full swing. All signs point to mobile devices steadily becoming even less expensive and more pervasive in the future. The mobile revolution and the explosion of digital content are impacting libraries and the services they offer, creating opportunities and challenges. Libraries can best meet these challenges—and best serve their mobile users—with a mobile services strategy that includes adoption of research-based guidelines and responsive design for development of its mobile websites.

APPENDIX 1: SUGGESTIONS FOR RESPONSIVE WEBSITE DESIGN

1. Start with a well-designed website for display on standard PCs (add accepted resolution) using a grid layout, and later add the necessary coding to display the website on mobile technologies.
2. Ensure that the design complies with the emerging research and evaluation guidelines. (A) Check ADA and Section 508 guidelines. (B) Follow the relevant guidelines from the National Cancer Institute's (NCI) Usability.gov website. While the guidelines were developed for health websites, the NCI staff recognized that the guidelines are applicable to most other informational websites. (C) Follow key research and evaluation guidelines: Ensure your website is easy for patrons to find when searching the web. Consider search engine optimization for the website. Ensure that it has a fast download. Note that fast downloads are needed. Designs with large files of pictures, audio, and video may slow download speeds. Responsive design requires programming using CSS3 and HTML5. Ensure that the site is not cluttered—users often abandon the website within fifty milliseconds of first viewing it (Lindgaard et al., 2006, p. 115). Ensure the text is legible (make design consistent [i.e., font selection]; make sure contrast is easy—no

patterned backgrounds, different colors for text and background; consider sans serif fonts—Verdana, Arial, or sans-serf fonts; provide functional equipment twelve-point fonts for body copy, since upward of 25 percent of college students often have trouble reading fonts on-screen; and avoid all boldface, caps, italics, and "fancy" fonts). (D) Use high sent links—that is, text links that are specific rather than general. (E) Avoid icon links. Users often fail to recognize what a link means. (F) Ensure easy navigation—standardize links (use the same color, formatting, etc.). (G) Provide a search function.

3. Run Google Analytics on your library web page to determine which sections patrons use more frequently.

4. Compare the design of the major website against the more frequently used pages based on the Google Analytics.

5. Review prior research on the frequency of use for various sections of library websites.

6. Run usability testing to identify major problems patrons might have with the website. (A) Know that usability testing is fraught with pitfalls for the unwary. (B) Check Usability.gov; it provides guidelines for running usability testing. (C) Seek out experienced usability testers. Consult psychology, journalism, communication, and computer science departments to see if any faculty members have expertise in usability testing.

7. Rearrange the home page website so that the more commonly used sections (key information) will be presented at the top of the mobile technologies.

8. Add needed coding for displaying the website on various screen resolutions once the basic website works—that is, sizes of mobile technologies.

9. Run the website through software that assesses responsive design that will be displayed on a variety of mobile technologies.

10. Check download speeds using software such as Dreamweaver.

11. Check the responsive-design website on all devices from PCs to mobile devices.

12. Check download speeds with various mobile devices and browsers in different locations.

13. Check the website with a variety of the mobile devices to ensure that it downloads quickly and displays the more often used information high on the display.

APPENDIX 2: SUGGESTIONS FOR MOBILE TECHNOLOGY INTERFACE DESIGN

User expectations of fast downloads:

- User expectations of download speeds for the initial website home page
- User expectations of the download speed for all subsequent sections of websites and elements, such as videos, still photographs, audio, and other features

Factors that influence users' first impressions of library websites:

- Which subsequent design features influence whether or not users are willing to use a library website and continue using it?
- What design features are critical?
- What content features are critical?

What factors influence the legibility of text?

- Fonts sizes and leading (spacing)?
- Font characteristics—that is, regular versus boldface, italics, all caps?
- Font colors?
- Font contrast with backgrounds?

What factors influence the legibility of icons?

- Size?
- Level of detail?
- Color combinations?
- Placement on page/screen?

What factors influence patrons' identification of icons—that is, meaning?

- Icon shape?
- Icon with text?

What influences the screen orientations that patrons prefer?

- When and why do patrons rotate mobile technologies between portrait and landscape orientations?
- Do design features need to change as orientations change? If so, how? In what ways?

What factors contribute to effective layout of websites displayed on mobile technologies?

- Are they different from desktop displays?
- How do layouts influence how patrons navigate a website?
- Do patrons' scrolling practices change when viewing a website on mobile technologies? If so, how? In what ways?

Do navigation strategies change when patrons use mobile technologies?

- What features clearly identify links?
- What contributes to writing high-scent links—that is, links that give patrons clues to content in different sections of a website?

How do patrons search—that is, what strategies do they use? How do these align with the structure and layout of a website?

- How long are patrons willing to search a library website?
- What factors make patrons abandon searching on a website?
- What factors discourage patrons to the point that they leave a library website?

What other factors will influence patrons' adoption of continued use of a library website?

  While the above items identify needed research applicable to mobile technologies, further research will identify other problems as research focuses more closely on mobile technologies.

REFERENCES

Adobe. (2014). Return on responsive web design. Adobe Experience Manager. Retrieved June 5, 2014, from http://www.adobe.com/.

Akamai Technologies. (2010). New study reveals the impact of travel site performance on consumers. Retrieved June 30, 2014, from http://www.akamai.com/.

Aldrich, A. (2010). Universities and libraries move to the mobile web. *EDUCAUSE Review Online.* Retrieved June 30, 2014, from http://www.educause.edu/.

Anderson, J., and Rainie, L. (2014). Digital life in 2025. Pew Research Center. Retrieved June 5, 2014, from http://www.pewinternet.org/.

Canalys. (2013). Tablets to make up 50% of PC market in 2014. Retrieved May 5, 2014, from http://www.canalys.com/.

Cervone, H. F. (2013). Managing digital libraries: The view from 30,000 feet; Selected practices and tools for better accessibility in digital library projects. *OCLC Systems and Services, 29*(3), 130–33. doi:10.1108/OCLC-05-2013-0015.

Chaparro, B., Shaikh, A., Chaparro, A., and Merkle, E. (2010). Comparing the legibility of six ClearType faces to Verdana and Times Roman. *Information Design Journal, 18*(1), 36–49. doi:10.0175/idj.181.04cha.

Choi, J. H., and Lee, H.-J. (2012). Facets of simplicity for the smartphone interface: A structural model. *International Journal of Human-Computer Studies, 70*, 129–42. doi:10.1016/j.iihs.2011.09.002.

Dahlstrom, E., Walker J. D., and Dziuban, C. (2013). *ECAR study of undergraduate students and information technology*, 2013. Retrieved June 25, 2014, from https://net.educause.edu/ir/library/pdf/ERS1302/ERS1302.pdf.

Dillman, D. A. (2007). *Mail and Internet Surveys*. Hoboken, NJ: Wiley.

Dobreva, M., O'Dwyer, A., and Feliciati, P. (Eds.). (2012). *User studies for digital library development*. London: Facet.

Dresselhaus, A., and Shrode, F. (2012, June). Mobile technologies and academics: Do students use mobile technologies in their academic libraries and are librarians ready to meet this challenge? *Information Technology and Libraries*, p. 82–101.

Durant, J. (2014, March 22). 5 reasons your responsive web design fails. *Business 2 Community*. Retrieved March 26, 2014, from http://www.business2community.com.

Everts, T. (2013). Rules for mobile performance optimization. *Communications of the ACM, 56*(8), 52–59. doi:10.1145/2492007.2492024.

Fox, R. (2012). Digital libraries: The systems analysis perspective; Being responsive. *OCLC Systems and Services: International Digital Library Perspectives, 28*(3), 119–25. doi:10.1108/10650751211262100.

Fox, S., and Rainie, L. (2014). The web at 25 in U.S. Research Center's Internet and American Life Project. Retrieved April 29, 2014, from http://www.pewinternet.org/.

Gatsou, C., Politis, A., and Zevgolis, D. (2011). Text vs visual metaphor and mobile interfaces for novice user interaction. *Information Services and Use, 31*, 271–79. doi:10.323/ISU-2012-0657.

Gayhart, L., Khalid, B., and Belray, G. (2014). The road to responsive: University of Toronto libraries' journey to a new library catalogue interface. *Code{4}Lib Journal, 23*, 1–17.

Hamilton, M. (2014). *Content authoring for responsive design*. Webinar for Society of Technical Communication members. Recorded May 28, 2014. Fairfax, VA: Society for Technical Communication. Retrieved June 9, 2014, from http://www.stc.org/.

Holtze, T. H. (2006). The web designer's guide to color research. *Internet Reference Services Quarterly, 11*(1), 87–101. doi:10.1300/J136v11n01_07.

Hu, R., and Meier, A. (2010). *Mobile strategy report: Mobile device user research*. California Digital Library. Retrieved June 30, 2014, from http://www.cdlib.org/.

Kim, B. (2013). Responsive web design, discover ability, and mobile challenge. *Library Technology Reports, 49*(6), 1–39.

Krueger, R. A. (2014). *Focus groups: A practical guide for applied research*. 5th ed. Thousand Oaks, CA: Sage.

Lin, Y.-C., Yeh, C.-H., and Wei, C.-C. (2013). How will the use of graphics affect visual aesthetics? A user-centered approach to website design. *International Journal of Human-Computer Studies, 71*, 217–27. doi:10.1016/j.ijhcs.2012.10.013.

Lindgaard, G., Fernandes, G., Dudek, C., and Brown, J. (2006). Attention web designers: You have 50 milliseconds to make a good first impression! *Behaviour and Information Technology, 25*(2), 115–26. doi:10.1080/0144929050030448.

Little, G. (2011). Keeping moving: Smartphone and mobile technologies in the academic library. *Journal of Academic Librarianship, 37*(3), 267–69. doi:10.1016/j.acalib.2011.03.004.

Llamas, R., and Reith, R. (2013). IDC finds worldwide smartphone shipments on pace to grow nearly 40% in 2013 while average selling price declines more than 12%. Retrieved May 5, 2014, from http://www.idc.com/.

Lumsden, J. (2008). *Handbook of research on user interface design and evaluation for mobile technology*. Hershey, PA: Information Science Reference.

Lynda.com. (2014). What do you want to learn today? Retrieved June 6, 2014, http://www.lynda.com/.

Mairn, C. (2013). Practical mobile design. In Peters, T. A., and Bell, L. (Eds.), *The handheld library: Mobile technology and the librarian* (pp. 85–94). Santa Barbara, CA: Libraries Unlimited.

Mangen, A., Walgermo, B. R., and Brønnick, K. (2013). Reading linear text on paper versus computer screen: Effects on reading comprehension. *International Journal of Education Research, 58*, 61. doi:10.1016.j.ijer.2012.12.002.

Marcotte, E. (2010). Responsive design. *A List Apart.* Retrieved June 30, 2014, http://alistapart.com/.

Nielsen, J. (2010, June 21). Website response times. *NN/g Nielsen Norman Group.* Retrieved June 27, 2014, from http://www.nngroup.com/.

Nielsen, J., and Budiu, R. (2013). *Mobile usability.* Berkeley, CA: New Riders.

Office of Citizen Services and Innovative Technologies. (2014). *DigitalGov.* Retrieved June 6, 2014, from https://www.digitalgov.gov/.

Pappachan, P., and Ziefle, M. (2008). Cultural influences on comprehensibility of icons in mobile-computer interaction. *Behaviour and Information Technology, 27*(4), 331–37. doi:10.1080/01449290802228399.

Parush, A., and Yuviler-Gavish, N. (2004). Web navigation structures in cellular phones: The depth/breadth trade-off issue. *International Journal of Human-Computer Studies, 60*, 753–70. doi:10.1016/j.ijhcs.2003.10.010.

Pearson Foundation. (2012). *Pearson Foundation survey on students and tablets 2012.* Retrieved June 30, 2014, from http://pearsonfoundation.org/.

Peters, T. A., and Bell, L. (Eds.). (2013). *The handheld library: Mobile technology and the librarian.* Santa Barbara, CA: Libraries Unlimited.

Pew Research Center. (2014). Pew Research Internet project. Retrieved June 5, 2014, from http://www.pewinternet.org/about.

Reidsma, M. (2014). *Responsive web design for libraries.* Chicago: American Library Association.

Rempel, H. G., and Bridges, L. (2013). That was then, this is now: Replacing the mobile optimized site with responsive design. *Information Technology and Libraries, 32*(1), 8–24.

Reuters. (2014). Smartphone sales growth to slow in 2014: Gartner. NDTV Gadgets. Retrieved May 1, 2014, from http://gadgets.ndtv.com/.

Robins, D., and Holmes, J. (2008). Aesthetics and credibility in website design. *Information Processing and Management, 44*, 386–99. doi:10.1016/j.ipm.2007.02.003.

Rossi, P. H., Lipsey, M. W., and Freeman, H. E. (2004). *Evaluation: A systematic approach.* 7th ed. Thousand Oaks, CA: Sage.

Saito, D., Saito, K., and Saito, M. (2010). Legibility evaluation with oculormotor analysis: The relationship between contrast and legibility. *Electronics and Communications in Japan, 93*(9), 27–33.

Sanchez, C. A., and Branaghan, R. J. (2011). Turning to learn: Screen orientation and reasoning with small devices. *Computers in Human Behavior, 27*, 793–97. doi:10.1016/j.chb.2010.11.004.

Schadler, T., Bernoff, J., and Ask, J. (2014). Re-engineer your business for mobile moments. *For CIO Professionals.* Forrester Research. Retrieved June 30, 2014, from http://www.forrester.com/.

Siegal, J. (2013). The post-PC era looks set to hit its stride in 2014. BGR. Retrieved May 5, 2014, from http://bgr.com/.

Smith, A. (2013, June). Smartphone ownership 2013. Pew Research Center. Retrieved May 1, 2014, from http://pewinternet.org/.

Stapleton, R. (2013). A new purpose; A new design: Welcome to the usability.gov re-boot. Usability.gov. Retrieved February 11, 2015, from http://www.usability.gov/.

U.S. Department of Health and Human Services. (2006). *The research-based web/design and usability guidelines.* Enlarged/expanded ed. Washington, DC: Government Printing Office. Retrieved June 5, 2014, from http://www.usability.gov/.

U.S. Department of Health and Human Services. (2014). Usability.gov: Improving the user experience. Usability.gov. Retrieved June 5, 2014, from http://www.usability.gov/.

Wilson, S., and McCarthy, G. (2010). The mobile university from the library to the campus. *Reference Services Review, 38*(2), 214–32. doi:10.1108/00907321011044990/

Zickuhr, K., Purcell, K., and Rainie, L. (2014). From distant admirers to library lovers—and beyond. Pew Research Center. Retrieved May 1, 2014, from http://www.pewinternet.org/.

Zickuhr, K., and Rainie, L. (2014, January). E-reading rises as device ownership jumps. Pew Research Center. Retrieved May 1, 2014, from http://www.pewinternet.org/.

Zickuhr, K., Rainie, L., and Purcell, K. (2013). Library services in the digital age. Pew Research Center. Retrieved May 1, 2014, from http://libraries.pewinternet.org/.

Zickuhr, K., and Smith, A. (2013, August 26). Home broadband 2013. Pew Research Center. Retrieved May 1, 2014, from http://pewinternet.org/.

Ziefle, M. (2010). Information presentation in small screen devices: The trade-off between visual density and menu foresight. *Applied Ergonomics, 41*, 719–30. doi:10.1016/j.apergo.2010.003.001.

Zimmerman, D. E., and Yohon, T. (2007). Small-screen interface design: Where are we? Where do we go? *IEEE Proceedings on Professional Communication*, 1–5.

Chapter Six

Essential Skills for Managing Electronic Resources in a Digital Campus Environment

Shannon Regan

The academic library, as an institution, is adaptable and ever changing within the constant evolution of higher education. Most notably, institutions of higher education have significantly changed with the advent of the Internet and reliable home Internet services. Distance-education programs and online classes are common tools for individuals seeking a customizable and flexible education plan; in consequence, academic libraries have adapted to fit the needs of the students in distance-education programs and classes. Electronic resources (ERs) and the building of electronic collections have helped influence the shift to distance and online education, as well as their expansion to support distance and online education. Managing these electronic collections in a digital campus environment, and providing the technical support to maintain access to electronic resources, spurred the creation of a new branch of librarianship and librarian: electronic resource management (ERM) and the electronic resources librarian (ERL). Electronic resource librarianship requires a complex set of skills to maintain a varied collection of electronic journals, databases, e-books, streaming media, online video, and whatever else may come their way. The focus of the chapter is on the day-to-day tasks an ERL manages in order to maintain an electronic collection. While assessment of ERs is discussed, collection building and collection development for ERs is outside the scope of this chapter.

UNDERSTANDING THE COLLECTION

Maintaining a collection of electronic resources is complicated by the fact that the collection is comprised of a myriad of different materials and is not a static collection. Unlike a collection of print monographs, in which the steps to adding a book to the collection have a clear and definite start and conclusion, ERs are fluid, and often the actual composition of the collection can change monthly, quarterly, and yearly. Electronic journals, e-journal packages, e-books, databases, and various other resources may have different acquisition cycles and require different review policies. The first step to successfully manage an ER collection across a digital campus environment is understanding what resources comprise the library's collection and their purchase model.

Electronic journals are typically licensed and offered via calendar-year subscriptions. While publishers, vendors, and aggregators may be willing to add an e-journal subscription midyear, the cost is prorated and review for continuing the subscription is based off of the calendar year, and not the year after the original start date. The window for reviewing e-journal subscriptions and making changes to packages of e-journals must be done several months before the new subscription year. Maintaining an accurate e-journal subscription list, and staying on track to review each title well before the new subscription year, will ensure that students and faculty have access to the titles the library has provided.

Managing and understanding e-book collections requires detailed record keeping and a clear collecting objective. Electronic books are offered to libraries with several different purchase models. Libraries may buy whole collections and titles and own those electronic formats in perpetuity, and they may subscribe to electronic collections and titles. In addition, e-books often have simultaneous user limits. A particular publisher may offer e-books with unlimited simultaneous user limits, while another publisher only offers a single simultaneous user. Detailed records of whether an e-book is leased or owned, has a simultaneous user limit, and is part of a collection is crucial for ensuring e-book access is maintained. Unlike e-journals, e-books are not necessarily licensed on the calendar year. New e-book subscriptions may start throughout the year and then have yearly subscription renewals for the year-to-date from the initial subscription start date. Like e-journals, leased e-books may be reviewed before the start of the new subscription year for cancellation or renewal. Accurate acquisition records of e-books' subscription renewal dates will ensure plenty of time for the review of e-books for renewal or cancellation.

Database collections and other electronic resource formats may not follow a predictable acquisition model. Databases and the resources that fall into the other category of ERs are typically licensed on a year-to-year subscription basis, with the possibility for multiyear agreements, and do not usually require a calendar-year subscription basis. Like e-books, these ER subscriptions may start throughout the year and then have yearly subscription renewals from the year-to-date to the initial subscription start date. Understanding the depth and breadth of a database and other ERs may prove time consuming for ERLs. Content included in a licensed database may change or update monthly, quarterly, or yearly. Records for implementing and tracking these changes and updates are one of the ERL's top priorities. Communicating these changes and updates to the public services staff will ensure that information is distributed to library users about any changes in the library's collection.

Academic libraries frequently license and collect electronic resources through shared consortia collections. Statewide, regional, or national consortia may negotiate for each individual library's behalf and make collections decisions for ERs on the collective bargaining power of a large deal. Understanding which materials in the collection are provided through a consortium is essential for maintaining access to electronic resources.

It is the ERL's responsibility to make sure collection-development librarians, subject specialists, and bibliographers have the information they need to make decisions about what ERs to continue for the new subscription year. For e-journals and e-books, this may mean providing the appropriate individual with a current list of titles paid from their resource fund, the appropriate usage data, and pricing information for the upcoming subscription year. It is not typically the ERL's responsibility to make these sorts of collection-development decisions, although it is not unheard of for an ERL to have a subject specialty and collecting responsibilities in addition to managing ERs.

Understanding what ERs currently comprise a library collection will help the public services staff and faculty better serve distance-education students. Access to ERs must be available when these students need them. The flexibility of online-learning and distance-education programs means that students may be doing research and schoolwork at odd hours. By maintaining detailed records and understanding the annual review of subscribed material, ERLs ensure that students have the resources they need when they want them. In addition, understanding what resources comprise the collection will enable the ERL to provide collection-development librarians with the information they need in a timely manner to make renewal or cancellation decisions for subscribed resources.

LICENSING ELECTRONIC RESOURCES IN A DIGITAL CAMPUS ENVIRONMENT

The Internet and electronic resources make providing research materials to distance-education students and remote users technologically possible. Over the past several years, it has become standard practice for publishers and vendors to provide remote access to electronic resources through a standard license agreement. It is through the license-negotiation process that ERLs advocate for the best practice of providing remote access to authorized students, faculty, and staff. When a new ER is selected for purchase, it is the ERL's responsibility to negotiate this agreement with the publisher and vendor, taking into consideration all the implications of serving distance-education students. The inability to come to an agreement on these terms usually results in the unfortunate circumstance where the library must walk away from an ER purchase or subscription. While unfortunate, there is no point in a library licensing electronic content that cannot serve the distance-education or online-learning population. Building relationships with publishers and vendors, and policies for the library's best practice in licensing electronic content, will ensure that this does not happen.

ERLs have been interjected into the license-negotiation process to ensure that libraries' specific terms of use are negotiated with regard to ER acquisitions. This is particularly important for libraries that serve a digital campus environment. Besides the necessity to provide remote access to ER collections, ERLs can also negotiate for electronic interlibrary loan, secure electronic transfer for interlibrary loan, inclusion of electronic resources in electronic reserves, and persistent URLs for faculty course information. These permissions are entirely outside the business scope of an acquisitions agreement but are crucial for the ability to serve distance-education and online-learning students. Working with the library's consortia to communicate individual institutional needs with regard to consortium-purchased electronic collections is crucial as well. Communicating these needs will ensure standard access and use across all collections.

As with understanding the depth and breadth of an ER collection, understanding the license agreements that govern the use of these resources is equally important. Reading through existing license agreements and reviewing them on an annual basis, along with the collection, will ensure the best possible terms of use and access. ERLs collaborate with the public services staff, subject specialists, the faculty, students, and other interested staff members to build a better understanding of how ERs are used in distance-education and online-learning programs. Incorporating the review of license agreements into the collection-development decisions for ERs will establish a culture of overall assessment of how resources support distance-education and online learning, and ways to improve the collection.

TRACKING AND PROVIDING ACCESS

Throughout this chapter, emphasis is placed on good record keeping for ERs. Tracking the subscription years, license terms of use, and renewal calendars for ERs is essential for ensuring uninterrupted access to these resources. There are a multitude of options for tracking electronic collections, and it constantly evolves with the advent of new ERs and new technologies. Successful tracking of electronic collections depends on the collaboration between many departments within the library system. It may include communication between technical services (acquisitions and cataloging), systems and web services, and public services. The position of ERLs may actually be located in any one of these departments. Understanding how ERs are tracked in any given library supporting a digital campus environment first requires understanding how each of these different departments plays a role in the electronic resource life cycle.

Before a new ER is purchased or renewed, the public services and collection-development librarians should review the resource for its relevancy. From there the ERL can begin the license-negotiation process to ensure agreeable terms of use. The ERL then collaborates with the acquisitions department to process the invoice. The ERL will be called on to confirm the pricing, subscription term or purchase agreement, and fund codes. Once payment is processed and access is available for an ER, the ERL then works with the systems or web services department to get the URL or other access permissions authenticated and discoverable. Simultaneously, the ERL may work with the cataloging department to ensure that the ER is displayed correctly in the catalog. Tracking the process from start to finish is the ERL's responsibility.

There is no right or wrong way to track electronic resources. There are commercial systems available via most integrated library system vendors called an electronic resource management system (ERMS). These products are marketed to integrate with a library's existing integrated library system to implement the seamless transfer of data between acquisitions, cataloging, and the ERL. In addition, a commercial ERMS typically serves as the back-end knowledge base for the point of access for library patrons via a website. Thus, it is possible to both track ERs and provide access from the same system. There are also open-source options for an ERMS; some libraries have built their own homegrown systems, or use Microsoft Excel or Access for maintaining their ER information.

Regardless of what type of system is used to track ERs, the information that needs tracking is consistent across the type of library and the type of content. There are seven standard components that an ERL should track carefully to ensure access to ER collections. These components are as follows:

Acquisition or purchase model. Cost, purchase or subscription, subscription term (calendar year or year-to-date), advance termination notice for cancellation (how much advance notice must you give a vendor or publisher before cancelling), from what fund the resource is paid, and the publisher or vendor.

License agreement terms. Tracking the term of the agreement, perpetual access rights, and the specific use permissions will ensure compliance with the license agreement.

Contact information for the publisher or vendor. This is extremely important for troubleshooting issues that arise with access to ERs, for changing the purchase model of a resource, or for negotiating an updated license agreement.

Access information. The URL with remote access specifications, the coverage date information for electronic journal subscriptions, any embargo information for resources in databases, simultaneous user limits, and any OpenURL linking specifications.

Administrative rights. Information for access to a vendor or publisher's administrative portal to access usage data, update contact information, update IP addresses, and download title lists or other information.

Usage data. Some ERMSs have the ability to track usage data as part of a resource record.

Notes. A notes field is helpful for tracking troubleshooting problems and resolutions, and general information.

Keeping in mind this is not a complete list, starting out by maintaining records for these components will help create a system to use for future reference. Tracking this much detailed information for electronic collections is helpful for maintaining uninterrupted access and to help collection-development librarians make collections decisions regarding electronic resources.

Integrating the detailed record information for access to ERs requires collaboration with the ERL and the library's systems or web services departments, public services, and cataloging. The design of the library's website will help facilitate how ERs are discovered. Understanding the best way for patrons to search for electronic content will involve conversations with public services librarians. Making it clear to distance-education and online-learning students how to access ERs from off campus is crucial for providing these students with the resources they need, when they need them. ERMSs may have web interfaces built into the knowledge base so that URL information and search and discovery boxes can be embedded in a library's web presence through a simple URL or widget. Libraries may choose to use these tools or build their own. It is the ERL's role to ensure that the information or data that feeds into these tools is up to date and accurate. Outdated URLs, or incorrect embargo information or coverage dates will display incorrect information or restrict access to users. In a digital campus environment, striving toward 24/7 service for ERs is only accomplished via accurate access information in the point-of-service tools. Including electronic collections in the library's catalog will involve conversations with the cataloging department. Striving toward consistent display of library ERs in the catalog will help users identify if a resource is available electronically and how to access it.

One final component of tracking and providing access to ERs is tracking perpetual access to e-journal subscriptions and in some situations e-books. Perpetual access is the right to access ERs from the years in which they were subscribed even if a subscription to that resource ends. It is also often called postcancellation access. If license agreements provide for perpetual access to resources for the years in which the library subscribed, tracking this information will ensure that access to those year's content remains discoverable through the library's discovery tools. If the library subscribed to an e-journal from 2009 to 2014 and decided to not renew for 2015, but had negotiated perpetual access rights with the publisher, that title should still remain accessible via a link with coverage dates listed as 2009–2014. Maintaining access to the ERs that the library has rights to is particularly important in a digital campus environment. Distance-education and online-learning students may not live near or have access to a robust research library. Thus, they may be solely reliant on the electronic collections provided via their educational institution. Ensuring they have access to all available materials will provide these students with the research materials they need to successfully complete their program or degree.

TROUBLESHOOTING

Inevitably, there will be an issue accessing a resource from the electronic collection. Parsing these issues, finding resolutions, and making updates to prevent these issues from reoccurring are some of the ERL's main duties. Preemptively, the ERL can communicate any updates in service that may require downtime on the provider's end, and other known issues with ERs to public services staff and on the library's website. This will give some forewarning to users that they may experience an access issue during this time. Developing a system for addressing ER-problem reports is crucial for ensuring distance-education and online-learning students can expect a timely resolution to a problem. Working closely with public services and access services staff to develop a policy that is in line with other library policies regarding issue resolution is crucial. It may be within the scope of your ability to respond and attempt to resolve ER-related issues the same day they are reported, but if public services and/or access services have different response times (within twenty-four hours, for example), library policy would not be consistent. Having consistent policies across all library departments will ensure users have clear expectations.

The first step to troubleshooting most ER problems is attempting to replicate the issue. If unsuccessful in replicating the problem, respond back to the user inquiring for more information, or see if the user is still experiencing the issue. If able to replicate the issue, an ERL can begin the process of determining the resolution. Some situations will be easy to resolve. Perhaps a distance-education or online-learning student is attempting to access ERs without authenticating through the library's website. A kind reminder to this individual about how to access resources from off campus may be all that is needed in that situation. Other issues may follow the path of known issues with known fixes, or may require more in-depth attention. Most importantly, follow up with the user to explain that you are working toward the resolution, and suggest some alternative resources the user may be able to use in the meantime.

Issues related to ERs can be extremely diverse. Preparing for each situation is not possible, but by having a policy for how to address ER issues, ERLs can manage these situations more effectively. Issues may range from an invoice that has not yet been paid so that the provider turned off access to an individual trying to access the collection with an outdated web browser, a lack of communication between the provider and library about a new access URL, or a simple misunderstanding on how to search effectively in an electronic database. In any of these situations, the ERL can endeavor to replicate the problem and resolve the issue, even if that means collaborating with other library departments or the provider in seeking the answer. As with other aspects of ER management, documenting issues with a particular vendor or resources will help track tendencies and significant downtime.

ASSESSING THE COLLECTION

Assessing the electronic resources collection in terms of how well it serves the distance-education and online-learning programs at a given institution goes hand in hand with understanding the collection. Looking beyond the collection-development considerations with regard to a particular resource (does it support the subject and program for which it was acquired?), ERLs can provide insight into if and how the negotiated terms of use best serve the needs of users, if the usage data reflects a meaningful justification for retaining a resource, and insight into how new purchase models could affect the collection development of electronic resources.

The existence of a collection-development policy may inform collecting decisions regarding electronic resources. Collection development librarians and subject specialists will be crucial for interpreting these policies and using them to make decisions regarding e-journals, e-books, databases, and other electronic content. The ERL can assist these librarians in making decisions by supplying ERs' specific data. The technology that supports electronic collections provided the opportunity to produce reliable usage data statistics. Most vendors and publishers can provide COUNTER-compliant data for how many times a collection or database is searched, how many times an e-journal article or e-book chapter is downloaded, how many pages are viewed in a collection, and other metrics. The COUNTER standard (Counting Online Usage of NeTworked Electronic Resources) was developed to allow librarians, publishers, and stakeholders to compare usage across different vendors and publishers. Usage data is typically available down to the month and may be downloaded and accessed via the vendor or publisher's administrative portal. This usage data may be used to determine the "cost per use" of an e-journal or e-book, and the value of an indexing and abstracting database. The ERL can assist collection development and subject specialists in interpreting this data. A collection-development librarian or subject specialist will know the size of an academic program, the scope of distance-education and online-learning programs, and the number of faculty members doing intense research, which will help an ERL determine good usage for an electronic resource. The difference in size of programs and the number of researchers in that subject area will skew how many people are using an electronic collection on a regular basis. For example, if your library serves a large biology department with distance-education and online-learning programs but a small computer science department with limited distance-education and online-learning programs, you can expect to see high usage on biology electronic collections and moderate usage for computer science collections. Determining what is or is not good usage data requires collaboration between an ERL and collection-development and subject specialists.

The analysis of usage data is only one piece of the assessment puzzle. Through this analysis it may be determined that a collection is being underutilized, or that a collection is not serving a program's needs. This information, in conjunction with resource costs, the library's mission, and new programs, may influence if certain electronic resources are renewed, cancelled, or marked for further review. Another aspect of ER assessment to consider is the number of issues experienced with resources in any given year. Documenting troubleshooting practices across the electronic collection will make obvious if any one provider or resource is underperforming in its ability to be accessible and trouble free. Electronic resources that are inaccessible, or plagued with issues, are particularly unfriendly to distance-education and online-learning environments. Assessing the issues related to these resources and the value of the resource is an integral part of ER assessment.

CONCLUSION

The intricacies of managing electronic resources in a digital campus environment vary and morph with unexpected, but dependable, frequency. Working in a digital campus environment, libraries and librarians have to be willing to adapt to these frequent changes and new realities. ERLs work diligently to take these issues in stride while maintaining a vast collection of electronic resources. Understanding the breadth and depth of this collection and making it usable for distance education and online learners is possible through careful licensing, detailed records, focused troubleshooting, and ongoing assessment. The combination of these skills will ensure that users in a digital campus have access to the resources they need, when they need them.

RESOURCES

Blake, Kristen, and Maria Collins. (2010). "Controlling Chaos: Management of Electronic Journal Holdings in an Academic Library Environment." *Serials Review* 36:242–50.

Bluh, Pamela M., ed. (2001). *Managing Electronic Serials*. Chicago: American Library Association.

Conger, Joan E. (2004). *Collaborative Electronic Resource Management: From Acquisitions to Assessment*. Westport, CT: Libraries Unlimited.

COUNTER. "Counting Online Usage of Networked Electronic Resources." http://www.projectcounter.org/ (accessed June 25, 2014).

Curtis, Donnelyn, Virginia M. Scheschy, and Adolfo R. Tarango. (2000). *Developing and Managing Electronic Journal Collections*. New York: Neal-Schuman.

Elguindi, Anne, and Kari Schmidt, eds. (2012). *Electronic Resource Management: Practical Perspectives in a New Technical Services Model*. Oxford, UK: Chandos.

Emery, Jill. (2013). "Techniques for Electronic Resource Management." *Library Technology Reports* 49, no. 2: 5–43.

Evans, G. Edward, and Margaret Zarnosky Saponaro. (2005). *Developing Library and Information Center Collections*. Westport, CT: Libraries Unlimited.

Fieldhouse, Maggie, and Audrey Marshall, ed. (2012). *Collection Development in the Digital Age*. London: Facet Publishing.

Fry, Amy, and Linda Rich. (2011). "Usability Testing for e-Resource Discovery: How Students Find and Choose e-Resources Using Library Web Sites." *Journal of Academic Librarianship* 37, no. 5: 386–401.

Gregory, Vicki L., and Ardis Hanson. (2006). *Selecting and Managing Electronic Resources*. New York: Neal-Schuman.

Hartnett, Eric, Eugenia Beh, Taryn Resnick, Ana Ugaz, and Simona Tabacaru. (2013). "Charting a Course through CORAL: Texas A&M University Libraries' Experience Implementing an Open-Source Electronic Resources Management System." *Journal of Electronic Resources Librarianship* 25, no. 1: 16–38.

Lipinski, Thomas A. (2013). *The Librarian's Legal Companion for Licensing Information Resources and Services*. Chicago: Neal-Schuman.

Mangrum, Suzanne, and Mary Ellen Pozzebon. (2012). "Use of Collection Development Policies in Electronic Resource Management." *Collection Building* 31, no. 3: 108–14.

Matesic, Gina D. (2009). "Every Step You Change: A Process of Change and Ongoing Management." *Journal of Library Administration* 49, nos. 1–2: 35–49.

North American Serials Interest Group. "NASIG Core Competencies for Electronic Resources Librarians." http://www.nasig.org/ (accessed June 25, 2014).

Pickett, Carmelita, Jane Stephens, Rusty Kimball, Diana Ramirez, Joel Thornton, and Nancy Burford. (2011). "Revisiting an Abandoned Practice: The Death and Resurrection of Collection Development Policies." *Collection Management* 36:165–81.

Poole, Julie. (2009). "Academic Branch Libraries: Assessment and Collection Development." *Journal of Library and Information Services in Distance Learning* 3, no. 3: 192–205.

Sheppard, Beth M. (2012). "Resource Use Patterns in a Distance Doctor of Ministry Population." *Journal of Religious and Theological Information* 11:138–57.

Warner, David. (2006). "Electronic Reserves: A Changed Landscape." *Journal of Interlibrary Loan, Document Delivery and Electronic Reserve* 16, no. 4: 125–33.

Whiting, Peter, and Philip Orr. (2013). "Evaluating Library Support for a New Graduate Program: Finding Harmony with a Mixed Method Approach." *Serials Librarian* 64, nos. 1–4: 88–98.

Chapter Seven

E-resources Workflows in the Age of Discovery

Amy Fry

Managing e-resources has always required ready adaptation to rapidly evolving standards and technology. The release and adoption of web-scale discovery tools beginning in 2008 has been another game changer for e-resources management and technical services. After adopting a discovery system, work such as licensing, record creation and loading, knowledge-base management, and troubleshooting transforms, and librarians must refocus existing e-resources management workflows around maximizing the utility of the discovery product. This chapter discusses models for e-resources management in the context of web-scale discovery, including approaches to staffing, training, documentation, assessment, and communication that can help libraries respond effectively to the complex demands of managing e-resources in the age of discovery.

E-RESOURCE WORKFLOW COMPLEXITIES

During the last decade, librarians have endeavored to establish workflows centered on the most important parts of the e-resources management process (Blackburn and Lowden, 2011, p. 63; Emery and Stone, 2011; ERMI 2 Steering Group, 2006; Weir, 2012, pp. 4–5). No matter how this process is described, each milestone in the life cycle of an e-resource encompasses a host of detailed activities, any of which, if missed, can cause access to the resource to fail, either immediately or at a crucial point for the patron (i.e., when accessing a resource from off-site or in using OpenURL linking). When one considers the number and variety of individuals and departments in the library who are involved in this work, it becomes even clearer what a delicate balance is involved in keeping electronic resources functioning and connected.

Even at libraries with fairly small technical services departments, work-flows surrounding electronic resources get complex quickly, and each step of every process requires lots of collaboration between staff members across units. This is why most authors agree that communication and creating a collaborative work environment are key to managing electronic resources successfully. At Bowling Green State University (BGSU) in Ohio, staff and responsibilities of technical services units intersect and overlap not only with each other but with the public services and information technology units as well. As shown in figure 7.1, the relationships of these units are better illus-trated by interlocking circles that represent where staff members share work and collaborate than by traditional charts that highlight unit divisions and reporting lines.

In launching WorldCat Local in 2008, OCLC (Online Computer Library Center) became the first company to create what is known as a "discovery layer": a central index that includes a library's bibliographic data as well as metadata about articles and digital material in its collection. The user inter-face for discovery layers relies on web search methods without the con-straints of traditional online public access catalog (OPAC) and online index searching. ProQuest's (formerly Serials Solutions) Summon followed World-Cat Local in 2009 (Elguindi and Schmidt, 2012, pp. 119–20), and EBSCO and Ex Libris began offering similar products soon after that.

As libraries began to adopt discovery technology, it became evident that adding a discovery layer adds a layer of complexity to the already highly complex e-resources management process. As illustrated in figure 7.2, add-ing discovery both adds new tasks within the e-resources life cycle and augments the scope of tasks already being performed. This is because the work of discovery is centered on a knowledge base and the publisher-defined collections it represents, rather than the OPAC and a library's locally defined collections cataloged item by item.

A representation of the universe of searchable information, knowledge bases initially inventoried only the contents of full-text journals in aggrega-tors and publisher packages to power OpenURL linking. In the discovery environment, knowledge bases now also represent non-full-text databases, collections of images, books, streaming audio and video, and more. They control not just journal lists and article linking, as they have for over a decade, but, now that they power discovery systems, also what patrons can find at the individual article, chapter, and image level in what is, most often, the primary access point to the collection. As a data source and tool, the accuracy and flexibility of the knowledge base, in terms of both what it includes by default and how it is customized and kept up to date at the local

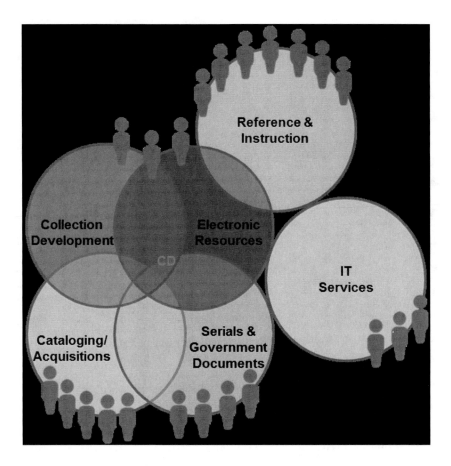

Figure 7.1.   Collaborative relationships of library units.

level by the technical services staff, is key to providing a successful discovery user experience.

Technical services units are the most appropriate areas to manage discovery technology because technical services librarians and staff members have experience managing large amounts of complex data, adapting to rapidly evolving technology for collection management (most of it add-ons or augmentations to the traditional integrated library system, or ILS), and (through the management of knowledge bases and OpenURL resolvers) linking collections previously siloed (Elguindi and Schmidt, 2012, pp. 110, 128; Somerville, 2013, p. 236).

Maria Collins (2009) identifies a number of ways that knowledge bases have impacted e-resources management, not the least of which is transforming technical services librarians and staff from item-by-item processor "prac-

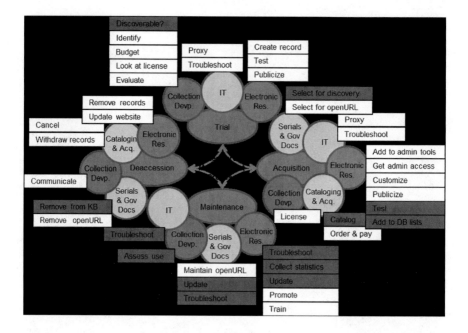

Figure 7.2.   Tasks in the e-resource life cycle with the addition of discovery.

titioners" to "managers of data sets at the macro instead of micro level" (p. 269). Implementing discovery further impacts e-resources management in the following ways:

- Selection and ordering. In the initial evaluation of a database, a library must ask if and how its contents can be discovered in its discovery layer, and it may decide not to purchase a product if the vendor does not have an agreement with the library's discovery vendor. User adoption of discovery tools is often so great that resources outside the scope of the discovery layer can fall in use dramatically after a discovery layer is implemented (Fry, 2014; Way, 2010).
- Receiving and maintaining. The acquisitions process for electronic materials (and, to some degree, print materials) must be altered after discovery implementation to add the steps necessary to select the material for discovery. This involves not only knowledge-base selection (even for resources that do not contain full-text books and journals) but also often further customizations within the knowledge base. For example, Summon provides a "database recommender" feature that requires the library to customize the linking URL, brief description, and keywords for each database selected in the knowledge base. In addition, databases must be prioritized for linking not only in the

OpenURL management system but also in the discovery layer. Names of databases and providers are often not standardized, which can make this process more difficult. Any changes to the database and provider require further changes in the knowledge base through the life of the resource; this can involve long follow-up times, as knowledge-base changes typically lag behind publisher changes, sometimes by many months. Any mistake in knowledge-base selection can cause a resource to be invisible in the discovery layer, which can have a huge impact on its use. Selection of e-book packages is particularly problematic, as publisher title lists and knowledge-base collection lists by package rarely match, and when purchases are made at a consortial level, it can be difficult or impossible for individual libraries to know which titles were purchased.

Troubleshooting. Testing and troubleshooting are greatly impacted by adding a discovery layer, which, because it is an add-on to the library's existing systems, provides another place where access can break down. Public services staff members often can't tell which system is causing a problem for a user, whether it is the proxy server, the OpenURL resolver, the knowledge base, the discovery layer, or the connections between any of these systems. Sometimes the problems are as specific as the way certain resources work when using certain versions of a specific browser. Staff members responsible for troubleshooting need an intimate knowledge of all the components as well as sophisticated problem-solving skills in order to identify a problem and who must be notified to fix it. Solutions can involve a wide variety of people, from internal library staff members to multiple vendors, and problems can require months of communication before they are fixed.

Assessment. Discovery layers impact resource use—driving up use of certain full-text products, causing drops in use to products outside their scope, and even impacting the use of print through the integration of HathiTrust data. Types of counts are also impacted—searches of individual products may drop even as their full-text downloads increase. After implementing a discovery tool, libraries must reexamine how they assess collection use and usage statistics.

Communication. Unlike the ILS environment, the discovery environment is one of frequent communication and collaboration between vendor and customer to tweak the functionality and user interface as the discovery product encompasses more content from more sources (Kornblau, Strudwick, and Miller, 2012, p. 154). In addition, since most data is not locally hosted, frequent communication about individual linking, metadata, and record problems is also normal. Rather than being focused on one data systems person, it is customary for this communication to be fairly distributed across the staff.

ORGANIZATIONAL STRUCTURE

Implementing discovery does not just change how library users find and access library collections—it also utterly transforms how library collections are integrated and requires a transformation in how resources are managed and how people work.

In a discovery environment, resources are more connected, so people (and their work) must be more connected too. Each module in the traditional ILS is isolated, and each function is separate, often requiring separate permissions for access and use. Isolating functions has the additional effect of isolating people's work (Fu and Fitzgerald, 2013, p. 54). The knowledge-base software that drives discovery is much more integrated, and this structure reflects the need for more integrated workflows to manage electronic materials. One source of tension in the current environment of e-resources management most certainly comes from the need to maintain and support the ILS (with its siloed approach to information and workflows) alongside discovery software within the same organization and with the same staff.

Integrated work requires adaptability and flexibility in organizational structure. Mary Somerville (2013) writes, "From the outset, the Web-scale discovery service life cycle required a new way of working that no longer depended on top down decision-making" (p. 238). If the decision to implement a discovery layer is the vision of an individual, he or she may not necessarily recognize the extent to which implementation will impact the work of librarians and staff members. When making decisions about discovery, leaders should be aware of the shift in work that will be required and communicate in ways that will result in broad buy-in from library personnel.

For example, when faced with the option to switch vendors for discovery, the library at BGSU took an entire year to carefully study the implications and work with the proposed software to know how a switch would impact not just the library's budget but also its workflows and, most importantly, the access to resources BGSU was providing its patrons. The final decision (to continue its Summon subscription) was made with input from staff members across the organization as well as from users. While it took a lot of work to reach a conclusion, the level of buy-in for the product and the library's decision made it one everyone could embrace.

WORKFLOWS AND DEPARTMENT STRUCTURE

While most experts believe e-resources work must be highly collaborative, there is no recommended model for staffing or workflow organization. Denise Pan (2012, p. 130) and Joan Conger (2004, p. 4) both stress that solutions must be local and will vary from library to library. Combining units and workflows as well as flattening organizational structures, however, are common strategies for workflow redevelopment (for example, see Beisler and Kurt, 2012; Branch 2012; Clendenning, Duggan, and Smith, 2010; Somerville, 2013). Collins (2009, p. 267) and Conger (2004, p. 8) both recommend centering electronic resources management in the position of an e-resources librarian who can lead collaborative teams and work with the staff across units to make sure information is shared.

At BGSU, the electronic resources librarian coordinates the completion of necessary tasks for e-resources management with librarians and staff members who specialize in serials, acquisitions, and collection management. These include record creation in the ILS (resource, license, contact, and bibliographic), knowledge-base selection (including any customizations or title-by-title selection for some packages), proxy setup, and testing (with proxy server, OpenURL resolver, and discovery layer), among other tasks. The technical services unit has made a concerted effort to share e-resources management knowledge across almost everyone in the unit by integrating electronic work into print workflows (a common strategy; see Collins, 2009, p. 266) and storing administrative information in ways that make it widely accessible. While some libraries cross-train staff, BGSU librarians have found duplicating knowledge of specific tasks in staff to be inefficient and instead cross-train on tools and create shared documentation in order to provide backup when needed.

Creating workflows collaboratively can be a good opportunity for an e-resources team to communicate (Beisler and Kurt, 2012, p. 109). At BGSU, a large team spent several months developing a detailed electronic resources acquisitions workflow soon after the electronic resources librarian position was added to the staff. While time-consuming, this gave the team the necessary opportunity to identify not only the details that had to be attended to every time a new resource was added but also who would be responsible for completing each task, which helped the team clarify the roles of each of its members. Workflows that include who should complete each task prevent the team from wasting time trying to decide who should do what (Branch, 2012, p. 326), or assigning people tasks who are not very familiar with them or who don't understand how they connect to other tasks. Later, when the library implemented Summon, team members had developed strengths and skills that helped them know where in the process for discovery their talents were most useful. A staff member who had formerly worked exclusively with serials now specializes in managing knowledge-base selections and keeping these up to date as well as troubleshooting linking failures (often connected to knowledge-base data). The coordinator of acquisitions and cataloging has the added responsibility of managing e-book records so they match and merge properly in the discovery environment. The electronic resources librarian makes customizations to package-level records in the discovery software (customizing features like the database recommender). Expansions to individual responsibilities such as these require each member of the team to have a sophisticated understanding of how the discovery layer works and how to manage resources so they work best within it.

Lenore England, Li Fu, and Stephen Miller (2011) recommend using checklists to keep each process, whether it is the acquisition of a resource or its cancellation, on track. Successful teams complete a "call and response" feedback loop about each task to keep projects moving forward (Collins, 2009, p. 262; Pan, 2012, p. 130): at BGSU, after a checklist is initiated for a particular process, the electronic resources librarian sends an e-mail to the e-resources team that lists which specific tasks need to be performed and who is expected to do each of them. Each team member responds to all when his or her part is completed. These responses not only aid accountability but also reinforce the collaborative nature of the work, even when each team member is completing his or her part independently.

Workflows should be detailed, listing all tasks that may need to be performed, while being flexible enough in execution to allow for individual modifications. This is because, as Pan writes, needing to make exceptions to procedures will be more common, in practice, than needing to complete every task outlined in a given procedure (Pan, 2012, p. 122). Workflows should also allow for quick recovery/alteration when they break down (which they certainly will; Branch, 2012, p. 326; Collins, 2009, p. 262). E-resources workflows are never complete. Once a process has been developed (usually to meet a certain need), something inevitably changes that requires the process to be revised or sometimes completely abandoned. This can be adding or discontinuing software, a change to a vendor interface or standard, or a subscription change at the local or consortial level. At BGSU, for example, the technical services staff collaborated with the library's IT services department to create a way to partially automate selection of a certain publisher's e-books in the knowledge base. Shortly after implementing this procedure, however, the OhioLINK consortium announced it would stop purchasing e-books from this publisher. In another example, librarians and staff members had just developed a detailed workflow for managing usage statistics when a change in the National Information Standards Organization's (NISO) COUNTER standard made the software being used with that procedure obsolete. The library adopted new software and with it an entirely new workflow only eighteen months later.

Eighteen months is standard for a change cycle in twenty-first-century libraries (Conger, 2004, p. 4). Developing workflows with the expectation of frequent revision and building time into the e-resources management process to account for their revision helps mitigate the frustrations of frequent change. Developing processes that build knowledge that can be deployed in similar circumstances also helps with this. For example, developing a process for managing e-resources statistics gave the staff the knowledge of standards and the information required to collect usage stats for all the platforms, making it much easier to implement a new process. Likewise, developing a process for extracting knowledge-base information from MARCit records is one that may be useful for other e-book collections in the future. Focusing on these successes helps make change more palatable.

TRAINING

In 2013, BGSU added a staff member to assist with electronic resources management, licensing, usage data collection, collection development, and support for a new institutional repository. Because BGSU's e-resources workflows are specific to its institution and staff, no training materials existed. Pan (2012) suggests employees learn by working through procedures with one another, and she also recommends "demonstrating and documenting procedures" as a training tactic (p. 134).

At BGSU, the new staff member and e-resources librarian worked through each e-resources management process with its existing documentation while the staff member recorded what was being done and who should do each task. After this, he updated the process's documentation and began writing out more detailed procedural workflows. This activity helped reinforce what needed to be done as well as brought out questions that remained. Lastly he used the revised documentation to work through the process a second time, with another resource, on his own. Often he didn't get all the way through the process the second time because he ran into unexpected problems or circumstances that had not been present with the first resource. This activity was repeated with four major processes: trial, acquisition, update/change, and cancellation.

One challenge with training for e-resources procedures is that many processes are done only a couple of times a year, and sometimes an example of a certain task is not available right away. Therefore, no matter how thoroughly a library tries to train on e-resources management processes, exceptions will come to light slowly for any new staff member. During training, it is less important to teach a person to complete the steps in a given workflow (since these will inevitably change from instance to instance each time they are done) than it is to teach about the e-resources themselves: what they are, where they come from, and how they work together. Understanding these fundamentals will help the staff know how to adapt procedures to deal with the many unique circumstances that will arise during each resource's life cycle. In the age of discovery, technical services staff members need to know how to create and analyze procedures in support of a big-picture goal, and learn independently how to use various tools, more than they need step-by-step instructions on how to do specific tasks or use specific tools.

FUTURE CHALLENGES

As Ping Fu and Moira Fitzgerald (2013) point out, "The traditional ILS does not have sufficient capacity to provide efficient processing for meeting the changing needs and challenges of today's libraries" (p. 47). Libraries have added more and more systems onto their integrated library systems to manage materials the ILS doesn't handle adequately, and not just subscription e-resources: BGSU has an Omeka instance and an institutional repository in addition to an electronic resource management (ERM), a knowledge base, an assessment product, and a discovery layer.

Libraries need one system that can accommodate all these content types and the information needed to discover them, administer them, and assess them. Right now libraries are moving toward unified staffing and work-flows—the next step is finally having unified systems (Han, 2012, pp. 166–67). Marshall Breeding has predicted that the next wave of library system migrations will be to cloud-based, next-generation systems such as Alma and Intota (Breeding, 2012). These are meant to manage bibliographic, discovery, patron, and administrative data about every item in a library's collection, digital and physical. As e-resources work becomes more knowledge-base focused and library collections become even more overwhelmingly digital, it only makes sense to manage physical items within the knowledge base instead of trying to manage electronic items within the ILS.

The cessation of duplicative processes will come with—or perhaps even before—this shift. At BGSU, for example, electronic resources are cataloged and receive ERM resource records. In addition, descriptions and keywords for them are added to the knowledge base for display in the discovery layer. Staff select journal and e-book titles in the knowledge base in order to purchase bibliographical records for them that are then loaded into the catalog, which in turn are loaded into the discovery layer, despite the fact that the knowledge-base selection makes them display in the discovery layer. These duplicative processes cover weaknesses in imperfectly linked add-on systems but ultimately will have to end. Some libraries have already stopped loading records from their knowledge base into their catalogs (Baxmeyer, 2011, p. 83) and are in the process of phasing out the public view of their ILS alto-gether. Many librarians still balk at taking this step, however, believing that the discovery layer does not provide adequate access to bibliographic records to facilitate the discovery of physical collections, particularly special collections. In the future, libraries will stop maintaining parallel and duplicative systems to provide access to collections, though most are not ready to take this step yet.

Another development libraries need is global, automated error discovery and correction for linking (Baxmeyer, 2011, p. 85). Currently, linking errors are reported one by one as they are discovered by users and librarians—if they are reported at all—and it is incumbent upon the library staff to log problem reports with the discovery vendor and content provider. This is an inefficient and reactive approach to database maintenance. ProQuest has taken steps to correct this in its new iteration of 360 Link: it includes a sidebar that allows users to switch to a different source if there's a problem with full-text linking, as well as a way for users to easily report a problem. ProQuest plans to track the problem reports and linking behavior for patterns that might indicate persistent problems with particular sources or providers, to adjust their metadata accordingly.

CONCLUSION

In the age of discovery, technical services workflows are no longer based on doing identical tasks to physical objects. They are now based on performing an individualized combination of tasks to a virtual object based on how it is obtained and how it will need to be accessed by end users. The people doing these tasks need an understanding of the variety of these collections (the breadth of their acquisition paths, accesses, and uses) and to be able, based on evolving professional knowledge and empowerment within their own positions, to make decisions on how to process each object. More than ever before, it is important to stay focused on how user paths to information influence processing. A focus on the user experience can provide the shared vision that feeds a culture of collaboration in technical services in the twenty-first-century library.

I would like to thank Linda Brown and Jeanne Langendorfer for contributing to this chapter by copresenting a session with me at the Academic Library Association of Ohio 2013 conference on this topic.

REFERENCES

Baxmeyer, J. (2011). In the "know": E-resource knowledge base management and best practices. A report of the ALCTS CCS Electronic Resources Interest Group meeting. ALA Midwinter Meeting, Boston, January 2010. *Technical Services Quarterly, 28*(1), 80–89. doi:10.1080/07317131.2011.524528.

Beisler, A., and Kurt, L. (2012). E-book workflow from inquiry to access: Facing the challenges to implementing E-book access at the University of Nevada, Reno. *Collaborative Librarianship, 4*(3), 96–116. Retrieved from http://search.ebscohost.com/.

Blackburn, J., and Lowden, S. A. (2011). Not for the faint of heart! A new approach to serials management. *Serials Librarian, 60*(1–4), 61–74. doi:10.1080/0361526X.2011.556439.

Branch, D. (2012). Electronic workflows: Taking it to the cloud. *Serials Librarian, 63*(3), 315–32. doi:10.1080/0361526X.2012.721739.

Breeding, M. (2012). Automation marketplace 2012: Agents of change. *Library Journal.* Retrieved from http://www.thedigitalshift.com/.

Clendenning, L. F., Duggan, L., and Smith, K. (2010). Navigating a course for serials staffing into the new millennium. *Serials Librarian, 58*(1–4), 224–31. doi:10.1080/03615261003625893.

Collins, M. (2009). Evolving workflows: Knowing when to hold 'em, knowing when to fold 'em. *Serials Librarian, 57*(3), 261–71. doi:10.1080/03615260902877050.

Conger, J. E. (2004). *Collaborative electronic resource management: From acquisitions to assessment.* Westport, CT: Libraries Unlimited.

Elguindi, A. C., and Schmidt, K. (Eds.). (2012). *Electronic resource management: Practical perspectives in a new technical services model.* Oxford, UK: Chandos.

Emery, J., and Stone, G. (2011). TERMS: What is TERMS? Retrieved from http://6terms.tumblr.com/.

England, L., Fu, L., and Miller, S. (2011). Checklist manifesto for electronic resources: Getting ready for the fiscal year and beyond. *Journal of Electronic Resources Librarianship, 23*(4), 307–26. doi:10.1080/1941126X.2011.627041.

ERMI 2 Steering Group. (2006). DLF electronic resource management initiative, phase II. Retrieved from http://old.diglib.org/.

Fry, A. (2014). The biggest winner: Using statistics to assess the effectiveness of an e-resources promotional campaign. *Journal of Electronic Resources Librarianship, 26*(1), 1–16. doi:10.1080/1941126X.2014.877330.

Fu, P., and Fitzgerald, M. (2013). A comparative analysis of the effect of the integrated library system on staffing models in academic libraries. *Information Technology and Libraries, 32*(3), 47–58. Retrieved from http://search.ebscohost.com/.

Han, N. (2012). Managing a 21st-century library collection. *Serials Librarian, 63*(2), 158–69. doi:10.1080/0361526X.2012.700781.

Kornblau, A. I., Strudwick, J., and Miller, W. (2012). How web-scale discovery changes the conversation: The questions librarians should ask themselves. *College and Undergraduate Libraries, 19*(2–4), 144–62. doi:10.1080/10691316.2012.693443.

Pan, D. (2012). Staffing changes to facilitate the shift to electronic resources. In R. O. Weir (Ed.), *Managing electronic resources: A LITA guide* (pp. 121–36). Chicago: ALA TechSource.

Somerville, M. M. (2013). Digital age discoverability: A collaborative organizational approach. *Serials Review, 39*(4), 234–39. doi:10.1016/j.serrev.2013.10.006.

Way, D. (2010). The impact of web-scale discovery on the use of a library collection. *Serials Review, 36*(4), 214–20. doi:10.1016/j.serrev.2010.07.002.

Weir, R. O. (Ed.). (2012). *Managing electronic resources: A LITA guide.* Chicago: ALA TechSource.

Chapter Eight

On the Brink of Linked Open Data

Evolving Workflows and Staff Expertise

Cory K. Lampert and Silvia Southwick

Digital libraries provide access to unique collections and contain a wealth of rich metadata describing these materials within library systems. As the library profession moves toward a future model of linked open data instead of closed silos of information, several implications arise for traditional staff roles and responsibilities. These include leading project design and development for linked-data investigations and evolving operational tasks such as management and creation of metadata into management and creation of data. This chapter builds on experience gained through the University of Nevada–Las Vegas (UNLV) Linked Open Data Project to examine and rethink workflows and staff skill sets necessary to transform traditional metadata work in digital libraries into sustainable creation of machine-readable data sets, in which information is expressed not as representative single items but as a vast number of triples in structured data. Because linked open data (LOD) is a relatively new and unexplored area for librarians, we start this chapter with a basic overview of the key concepts necessary to understand this topic and explain how these have initiated new ways of thinking in digital libraries. Next, we discuss the implications of practical work in this experimental area and provide an overview of an academic library project broken down into phases. Finally, competencies and skills are aligned with the phases of the project, and general recommendations for preparing the staff to work with linked open data are provided.

LINKED OPEN DATA CONCEPTS

LOD is a departure from current practice because it requires embracing several core principles—first established by Tim Berners-Lee (2006)—that, when applied, move beyond metadata records encapsulated in systems to a more flexible world where machine-readable statements can be linked together revealing relationships and context for users. The following concepts are key to understanding the principles:

- uniform resource identifier (URI)
- Triples using the *subject-predicate-object* syntax to form statements
- HTTP Protocol
- Resource Description Framework (RDF)
- Triplestores
- SPARQL

First, one needs to use URIs as identifiers for "things" (photographs, manuscripts, places, people, corporate bodies, etc.). Second, one needs to provide those things with their assigned URIs, expressed in triples using a serialization of RDF. The RDF triples are stored and managed in a triplestore with associated software and a server. To be truly "open" linked data, and to comply with Berners-Lee's principles, the data set must also be published so that others can use it. The linked-data query language SPARQL can then be used to retrieve search results against integrated data sets, including the locally produced LOD and other published LOD from diverse repositories.

This chapter does not seek to explain all concepts related to triples, RDF, and the query language SPARQL, but rather these are mentioned to provide a foundation of essential concepts relevant to this new framework of data management. There are many resources freely available for those new to linked data. Readers seeking a basic overview may be interested in an article we published in 2013: "Leading to Linking."

Another approach to comprehending LOD is to think of information on a scale using the five-star data chart (also presented by Berners-Lee, 2012). Data is classified on this scale according to its degree of usefulness, openness, and interconnectedness. The lowest level on the scale could be a scan of a document containing facts/content/information contained in an image file. The content may be understandable to humans, but it is not usable by machines. Moving along the scale, the content could be extracted and added to a machine-readable structured format (like a spreadsheet) making it more useful, but if the information is in a proprietary spreadsheet format, it is not interoperable across platforms. To achieve interoperability, the content could be taken out of proprietary software and delivered in an open format. In addition, it could have a URI assigned and be delivered as an RDF file, making it possible for others to point to and reuse the information. The "five star" level would mean that content is completely transformed into machine-readable, structured data and is presented in a nonproprietary format, using URIs and linked to other data sets. These concepts are applied and in use by a growing number of data creators from the LOD cloud, a web of rich, reusable, interconnected data that is revolutionizing commerce and technology fields and has great potential for education and cultural heritage.

Libraries, archives, and cultural heritage institutions holding unique materials are positioned to make important and rich contributions to linked data due to the rare nature of their materials and the potential of their collections to reveal interesting relationships. Many in the field are monitoring, participating in, and contributing LOD data to this movement, and several initiatives—such as the W3C (2010) Library Linked Data Incubator Group and the Linked Open Data for Libraries, Archives and Museums (LODLAM) community (http://lodlam.net/)—have made great progress to increase collaboration and education across the library and cultural heritage fields. This has resulted in excitement about new possibilities and widespread interest in the implications for libraries, but only a small proportion of the published literature and LOD documentation deals with practical applications of LOD in digital libraries. Making the jump from theory to practice in linked data demands a steep learning curve, thoughtful project design, and a close examination of current practice. This chapter will focus on these areas to provide insight and recommendations for those considering adoption of LOD for their collections. Advice will be most relevant to digital library managers and those engaged in work with unique physical collections and archival materials. LOD is only beginning to be adopted across the digital library field, and there will be a period of transition as repositories begin to transform their metadata, but it is useful to begin conceptualizing projects and rethinking current workflows where one can perform actions to prep the data and ready it for the next era of LOD.

IMPLICATIONS OF EVOLVING TO LOD

Evolving from traditional metadata creation into a space of LOD creation has several implications for digital library managers and their organizations. These fall into the following areas:

- Establishing LOD as strategic goal in the organization
- Acquisition of knowledge: LOD concepts, best practices, skills sets, training, and so forth
- Designing LOD projects, case studies, and workflows for local processes
- Operationalizing new workflows and supporting evolution of staff roles

- Assessment of LOD work
- Sharing with LOD community

Strategic Planning

Before beginning any revision of workflow or practice, digital library managers and their administration will need to consider the benefits of adopting linked data and decide to embrace the experimental nature of this new area. It can be helpful to outline a philosophy that will guide their program's strategic approach to LOD depending on resources and priorities. Staff at University of Nevada–Las Vegas (UNLV) Libraries started out with a low-risk discussion group and, as knowledge developed, communicated the need for a more resource-intensive project. The initiative was prioritized during library strategic-planning processes, and rationale were established to guide the work. Three core ideas that helped to shape the case for LOD investigation are as follows:

- Explore freeing data from silos so that users can see the power of LOD.
- Commit to adopting an approach that preserves richness of data in the transformation process by controlling this step locally rather than depending on vendors or other digital library aggregators to do it.
- Embrace fully the collaborative nature of LOD.

Acquisition of Knowledge

At time of publishing, library-linked data is in its first wave, and any practical approach will require a spirit of experimentation and investigation. That said, a careful consideration of the large body of literature is of paramount importance for a successful project. Strong grounding in linked-data concepts is the first step, but as projects are designed and developed it is also important to be rigorous in evaluating tools and models for project adoption. By adhering to common models and sharing knowledge of tools and technologies, individual projects will achieve better results and the entire LOD community benefits. As with any new area of exploration, projects will require decision making, testing, and revision. Embracing the spirit of learning by doing can be a helpful attitude when diving into the world of LOD.

Project Design

Much theory is known, and LOD is a prolific area of research, but less is known about practical application. Librarians and archivists serve as leaders in many aspects of collections and access, yet very few are leading LOD projects. Work is needed in areas of transformation of metadata, creation of ontologies, and development of user interfaces, just to name a few. Because these projects will need to be defined and developed, staff will need to provide leadership, secure support and resources, provide technical project management skills, and be able to document and communicate results. Often, this work will be in addition to their "regular" job. Academic libraries and organizations that support case studies and LOD research will have a major impact on the implementation of LOD and will have a much louder voice in the way the community develops and the outputs that are created. Establishing goals within every project design will keep the project on track and provide indicators of success.

Operationalizing New Workflows

But as more digital libraries work in the area, there will be less risk, more research and development, and more engagement among individuals and collaborative groups including concrete recommendations and training opportunities. Digital library staffs already have a commitment to increasing access to materials, so what is most needed is support from managers to evolve their employees' skill sets to accommodate the opportunities of LOD. Key positions in metadata creation will change drastically when LOD is the norm, but in the meantime, managers need to slowly ramp up staff training within the larger context of library priorities. One of the most important areas to begin work immediately is to analyze data being created in digital libraries and begin to enforce stricter standards for interoperability and consistency. The focus of metadata managers will need to be expanded in the world of LOD. No longer are they solely focused on the creation of collection-level or even item-level records. They also need to work on thinking in a broader way about what relationships are present in the data and work to identify "things" (triples) related to the "thing" (triple) being created. This deconstruction of metadata records into triples requires a fundamental shift in approach.

Assessment

To reap benefits from LOD experiments, projects, and investigations, project goals should be evaluated during and at the conclusion of the work. One of the most important aspects of LOD work at the project phase is to document decisions made and record results. For instance, even if a technology tool is evaluated and abandoned for an alternative, writing up the rationale and testing can be of benefit to others in the community. There are many possible deliverables from an LOD project; anything from a cleaned-up vocabulary to a large, published data set. The newness of this area should encourage experimentation as well as the assessment of experiments undertaken.

Sharing with the LOD Community

The term "LOD" practically says it all. The LOD community is one that seeks to make connections and share openly. To participate in LOD is to be a part of a community, and communities are made up of contributors. First and foremost is the concept of sharing data. This is a change in thinking for some metadata providers, because it means designing data for reuse. Publishing data requires giving up control and letting others take, edit, and use "your" data. But LOD only fulfills its promise if data is shared and can be linked across repositories, a fundamental philosophy that will ultimately benefit users. In addition, since many LOD tools are open source, libraries need to reframe their expectations away from dependence on passive technical support to embracing a more dynamic relationship as good citizens in the culture of sharing and problem solving.

COMMON METADATA CREATION WORKFLOW

Before discussing the UNLV project and detailing the phases involved in LOD creation, it is important to establish the current practice in digital libraries that allows one to describe one's materials. Creation of metadata for digital collections usually follows common steps such as those shown in figure 8.1. This chapter assumes a basic knowledge of metadata workflow in traditional metadata creation, including attributing identifiers, capturing technical and preservation metadata, assigning descriptive metadata, and using controlled vocabularies. The workflow in figure 8.1 shows the digitization process and the main steps for creating metadata for a photographic print. Note that this workflow can be adapted depending upon the type of the material being described, the software and hardware that is being used, or even the metadata schema being adopted (for example, the schema might not include preservation metadata). The purpose here is to provide a picture of current practice to better show contrasts with LOD workflows. In the foreseeable future, most digital libraries will not be able to fully adopt an LOD process to replace current metadata practice. Therefore, this figure also serves as a reminder of the parallel process that may continue to be carried out, even as work evolves to accommodate LOD.

OVERVIEW OF THE UNLV LOD PROJECT

Commonly, LOD projects, as with any other project, go through traditional phases of project development such as planning, design, and implementation. Due to the nature of LOD, we add two more phases: publishing and consuming the LOD. The concern in developing this project was to build a system

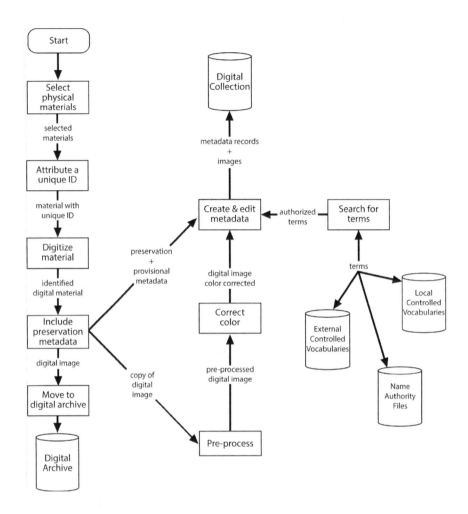

Figure 8.1. Common digital collection metadata creation workflow.

that operates smoothly and is integrated, as much as possible, with current metadata creation workflow. We use the term "system" in a broad sense, meaning that it refers not to a single software application but to a series of processes that might include user input and might run in one or more applications but at the end will produce LOD.

By taking a closer look at the UNLV's LOD project, we can see the interest is in identifying the processes that might affect current metadata workflows or that require special skills. In order to provide readers with some context, we present a brief overview of the main actions associated with each phase of the project.

For the purpose of this chapter, we have separated the decision-making processes necessary for developing this project from workflows and the actual operation of the tools selected to achieve the goal of publishing LOD. By making this clear distinction, we were able to identify sets of skills needed for those involved in conceptualizing and developing the project and for those responsible for day-to-day operations. Table 8.1 shows inputs and outputs for each phase of the project.

Note that work on the project led to the selection of specific technologies for performing transformations of metadata into linked data. We also devised and documented procedures associated with these technologies to generate and publish LOD. Later in this chapter, we present workflow for this operational aspect of the transformation.

Documentation is essential, and it should be developed throughout all phases of the project, as shown in table 8.1. The field of linked open data is relatively recent, and it has been evolving at a fast pace. It is critical to document processes and decisions made to create and maintain linked data. Documenting allows more efficient trainings and process revisions, when necessary. A brief explanation of project phases follows.

Table 8.1.   Phase inputs and outputs.

Inputs	Project phases	Outputs
Linked data literature	Planning phase	Concepts and best practices applicable to digital collections
Concepts and best practices applicable to digital collections	Design phase	Local URI structure; rules to assign URIs; selected model: Europeana data model
Digital collections metadata schema; Europeana data model; linked data technologies	Implementation phase	Mapping between metadata schema and Europeana data model; selected technologies; design on how to operate transformations into linked data
Triplestore technologies and their user manuals; linked data best practices	Publishing phase	Selected technologies; information on how to publish LOD
Data visualization tools	Consumption phase	Selected technologies; information on how users and machines can access LOD

Planning Phase

The first phase of the project refers to a thorough literature review to understand linked-data concepts and their applications and technologies available to support LOD generation. At UNLV, this was accomplished through the creation of a study group where participants were volunteers from diverse areas of the University Libraries. Once basic knowledge of linked-data concepts and the major goals had been acquired, the UNLV team designed a project.

Design Phase

The design of the project was based on what was learned from the planning phase. The literature review indicated that various decisions were needed up front. The main ones are as follows:

- Identifying the type of "things" described in the digital collections (for example, materials from Special Collections, people, corporate bodies, etc.)
- Defining local URI structure
- Specifying rules to assign URIs to "things"
- Selecting or devising a data model prescribing the predicates to be used for each class of "things"

These decisions need to be expressed in written documents to serve as guidance for decision making during the implementation phase.

While selecting an existing data model to guide transformation of metadata into LOD would be ideal for interoperability purpose, the reality is that there are not many to choose from. The Europeana Data Model (EDM) was particularly helpful for the UNLV team, but it has limitations. EDM might not be as helpful for those digital collection managers who are adopting the Encoded Archival Context—Corporate Bodies, Persons and Families standard (EAC-CPF). This standard is highly hierarchical and covers much more detail concerning corporate bodies, persons, and families than the EDM model. So, in cases where data models or ontologies are not available for specific standards, it would be necessary to create one. This would require specialized skills and might need different types of technologies.

Implementation Phase

This phase refers to the specification of processes for transforming metadata into linked data using decisions made during the design phase. The outputs of the implementation phase are the chosen technologies and the documentation on how to use the selected technology to generate LOD.

During this phase, the UNLV team examined a few technologies and selected OpenRefine, which seemed the easiest to operate and includes functions to map metadata to the chosen data model. The UNLV team performed various tests with the technology, simulating the transformation using actual metadata extracted from UNLV's digital collections. The various tests conducted with metadata allowed the team to refine the current workflow for metadata creation in order to increase metadata quality, facilitating the transformation into linked data.

In terms of technology for the transformation of EAC-CPF into linked data, one may need to evaluate technologies that facilitate the work with hierarchical data structure, such as Karma.

Publishing Phase

For the publishing phase, there are at least two options for making linked open data available on the web:

- Create dumps (RDF files) of your data sets and make them available on the web.
- Upload the RDF files to a triplestore that is also a SPARQL endpoint, making your data sets available on a server connected to the Internet.

In both cases, users or other data providers will be able to query the data and even harvest the data to be aggregated to their own data sets. The UNLV team opted for offering the LOD through a triplestore SPARQL endpoint. The main action for publishing refers to uploading RDF files into a publically available triplestore.

Consumption Phase

For the consumption phase, the UNLV team experimented with different visualization tools to display the LOD. The first experiment was with the Pivot Viewer, which was installed in the OpenLink Virtuoso server. This visualization tool was particularly helpful to show materials that have appealing images. It allowed users to interact with a preselected set of images (via SPARQL) in diverse ways.

Two other experiments were done with the open-source software Rel-Finder. In the first experiment, the team displayed relationships among people identified in oral history interviews. The user interacts with the interface by indicating people between whom they would like to display relationships. The network of relationships is dynamically constructed, and users have the ability to add or eliminate people from the list of people whose relationships are being displayed.

The other experiment displayed relationships among people and other *things* represented in the data set. For example, looking at the relationship among Frank Sinatra, Dean Martin, and Sands Hotel and Casino, the system showed various photographs depicting these two artists in a show rehearsal at Sands Hotel.

As a next step in the consumption phase, the UNLV team will develop an interface to search and display the data as well as data from other relevant data sets. While this interface has yet to be developed, the entire process for transforming metadata into LOD was established and ready for operation.

SYSTEM OPERATION

The workflow in figure 8.2 is a simplified representation of the operation process that needs to be activated every time a new collections or new records of a collection are being transformed into LOD. For a better understanding of the functions necessary for transforming metadata into LOD, a brief description of these steps follows.

The first step in the workflow is to clean the metadata. This process is a core activity in the everyday lives of metadata librarians. In terms of LOD, the focus is on rigorous adoption of controlled vocabularies, that is, only terms in the controlled vocabularies should be used in the digital collections records, respecting the term's format and spelling. This is essential for using automatic reconciliation processes.

For increasing interlinking with other data sets, when there is no authorized name for a person or corporation being recorded, it is necessary to look for these names in other data sets. If the person or corporation being described is included in a data set, it is best practice recommendation that the metadata creator would adopt the names used there and reuse their corresponding URIs. If other data sets don't refer to the target person or corporation, local controlled vocabularies should be used to record the corresponding name and a local URI be assigned to this person or corporate body.

After cleaning, the next step is to prepare metadata to be transformed into LOD. Preparation is needed in particular situations. For example, if names follow the Library of Congress Authority files format, personal names need to be separated from birth and death years. One might need to eliminate extra spaces in field contents, merge similar terms that refer to the same concept, and so on. In the UNLV project, the preparation of the metadata is performed using OpenRefine. This process might involve string manipulations and therefore requires staff to have knowledge of the tools to do so. For example, OpenRefine allows the use of a specific tool to manage strings, which is similar to regular expressions, a well-known tool for programmers.

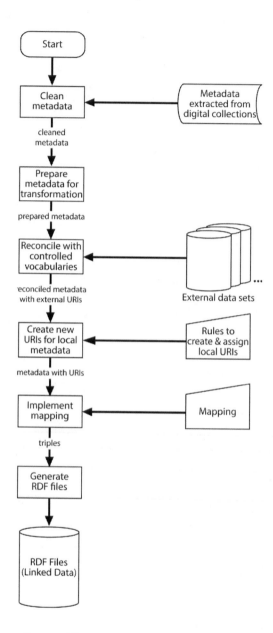

Figure 8.2.   Operation workflow.

Following this preparation, the team needs to recover corresponding URIs for the fields that are controlled by vocabularies or name authority files. This is called reconciliation. Some technologies, such as OpenRefine, automate this process. The reuse of URIs is essential to enable linking within and across data sets. Once reconciliation is performed, it is necessary to create local URIs and assign them for those terms that were not matched during the reconciliation.

As a rule of thumb, local URIs also need to be assigned to the materials being described (assuming that these materials are unique and do not have a corresponding URI).

Management of URIs is a new task for librarians. It requires the adoption of robust rules for creating and assigning new URIs. It should be accompanied by a systematic process for recording which URIs are assigned to which things. In addition, the process of managing URIs should generate lists of special statements (triples) to indicate when a local URI is the same as another URI that was created for the same thing, if such a latter URI exists and was identified.

Once all *things* have their corresponding URIs, the actual transformation should be implemented guided by the mapping. This process should be supported by technology. OpenRefine is used for this task in the UNLV project. Another common solution to perform the transformation is to develop XML style sheets to accomplish this task. As result of the transformation, triples are generated following the RDF framework. The RDF files are then generated.

Note that the workflow shown in this section is simplified and does not apply to all situations. In the UNLV project, a flat metadata structure determined the procedure. When dealing with hierarchical schema such as Encoded Archival Description (EAD) or EAC-CPF, these workflows should be revised. We believe that as LOD starts to become more widely adopted, these functions will be gradually incorporated into digital asset management systems. For this particular project, the majority of the functions necessary to produce linked data were not available in the current digital asset management system, CONTENTdm. The UNLV team had to use different technologies for the implementation and publishing phases.

Maintaining RDF files is a task that might be executed with the support of a triplestore. RDF files are kept in named graphs inside triplestores. Graphs are a way to organize data facilitating its maintenance. At this point, the UNLV team has been creating graphs for each of UNLV's digital collections. Using the SPARQL language, one can search within or across graphs. Rules for naming and creating graphs are also necessary to be created to more efficiently manage RDF files.

The SPARQL language, besides querying data at local triplestores, or in distributed data sets, has many other important functions related to the management of graphs and RDF files. A major challenge in managing RDF files is to maintain their synchronization with the digital collections (assuming that these are separate systems—parallel structure). The British Library, for example, maintains a synchronization system that is not in real time. Periodically the data set is regenerated and uploaded in their triplestore. In smaller intervals of time, they update their triplestore with triples generated from new records added to their catalog.

While most of the work needed for generating and maintaining LOD can be done by librarians, it is important to secure support from the library technology staff when adopting open-source technologies or more complex database management systems such as OpenLink Virtuoso. Ideally at least one professional from information technology (IT) should be part of the linked-data project team.

PREPARING THE STAFF FOR LOD

We present below some of the most important competencies required for those who plan to design a linked-data project or for those planning to work on the operation of a linked-data system. As different competencies may be needed depending on the phase of the linked-data project, these are aligned with each phase, as shown in table 8.2. Most of these competencies were acquired during the project development. It is not necessary to have all prior to starting, but we share them in the hopes that they will be helpful in planning and forming a successful project team.

CONCLUSION

LOD is happening right now, and it is certain that in the twenty-first-century library, shareable and machine-readable data will serve a role. There are many benefits to this approach, including more robust discovery experiences for users. As libraries begin to align staff roles to this new function, it is important for managers and administrators to understand implications present in this work and design LOD projects that wisely leverage their available resources. With a more concrete understanding of LOD project design and operational tasks, gained from the UNLV Linked Open Data Project, the shift from a focus on collections and records can be more easily imagined across a range of digital libraries. Staff will need to take the necessary step to educate themselves about the concepts of LOD, but in the same way libraries evolved to the online public access catalog, LOD will offer new opportunities for those who embrace the future. Concrete skill sets and personal qualities can be identified now to help guide organizations to develop their human resources along with their strategic and technological resources.

Table 8.2.   Alignment of phases and competencies.

Stage	Competencies	Personal qualities
Planning phase	Extensive experience using IT (does not require development skills); knowledge of databases; management skills (white paper); writing skills	Open minded to innovation; motivation to learn; strategic thinking (sell the project); detail oriented; feel comfortable with uncertainty; ability to work in teams; user focused
Design phase	Ability to analyze complex technical problems; experience evaluating technology; analytical skills to interpret technical documentation; experience testing and troubleshooting systems or code; experience documenting processes	Organized; ability to navigate between large picture and details; ability to apply theory to practice; ability to translate complex technical details to nontechnical stakeholders
Implementation phase	Extensive experience with IT; experience with databases; understanding of the http protocol; knowledge of the content of digital collections; experience with mapping (e.g., mapping for harvesting); knowledge of the data model being developed	Detail oriented; grounded in best practices (both metadata and LOD); self-guided learner; committed to benefits of linked open data; willing to consult LOD community for guidance
Publishing phase	Knowledge of databases; familiarity with SPARQL language; understanding of RDF graphs; awareness of other LOD sets	Technically fluent in (or able to learn to discern) software functions applicable to project; active participant in LOD community and open-source software communities
Consumption phase	Comprehensive knowledge of the SPARQL language; experience using application programming interfaces (APIs); design skills; web-development skills	Creative; experimental and iterative; user focused

Stage	Competencies	Personal qualities
System operation	Experience with IT; experience with CVs; search skills; knowledge of collections and content	Ability to adapt current skills to new functions; motivated to innovate; detail oriented; value high-quality data; analytical skills (identify relevant data sets); willing to provide feedback to improve the system

REFERENCES

Berners-Lee, Tim. (2006). Linked Data. Retrieved from http://www.w3.org/DesignIssues/LinkedData.html, para. 1.

Berners-Lee, Tim. (2012). 5 Star Open Data. Retrieved from http://5stardata.info/.

Europeana. (2011). EDM Primer. Retrieved from http://pro.europeana.eu/edm-documentation.

Lampert, Cory K., and Silvia B. Southwick. (2013). Leading to Linking: Introducing Linked Data to Academic Library Digital Collections. *Journal of Library Metadata, 13*(2–3), 230–53. Retrieved from http://www.tandfonline.com/.

W3C Incubator Activity. (2010). W3C Library Linked Data Incubator Group. Retrieved from http://www.w3.org/2005/Incubator/lld.

Index

About the Contributors

Suzanne Chapman is head of the User Experience Department and a senior associate librarian at the University of Michigan Library.

Ian Demsky is web content strategist and an associate librarian at the University of Michigan Library.

Amy Fry has been an academic librarian since receiving an MS in library and information science from the University of Illinois at Urbana–Champaign in 2003. She has been the electronic resources coordinator at Bowling Green State University since 2009, where she is also the librarian for the School of Art. Her research interests include usage patterns, resource discovery, and search behavior related to online resources; electronic resources workflows and management models; and website usability. She has published in the journals *portal: Libraries and the Academy*, the *Journal of Academic Librarianship*, and *Serials Review*.

April Grey is the catalog librarian at Adelphi University in Garden City, New York. She completed her masters of library science degree at the University at Buffalo. Grey serves on the American Library Association Diversity Committee and the Programming Review Task Force for the Association for Library Collections and Technical Services.

Rachel Isaac-Menard is the reference/web services librarian at Adelphi University in Garden City, New York. She is also head of research support and reference for *Architecture_MPS*, a peer-reviewed journal. She completed her masters of information studies degree at the University of Toronto.

Cory K. Lampert is the head of digital collections at University of Nevada–Las Vegas Libraries, where she is responsible for operations and strategic planning for a dynamic department that comprises digitization facilities, several digital collections systems/technologies, and five permanent staff. She manages several collaborative digital initiatives, including conceptualizing, writing, and implementing grant-funded digitization projects. Lampert's research interests are in the areas of linked data, strategic planning for digital libraries, and mentorship of staff. She received her MLS from the University of Wisconsin–Milwaukee and her BA from Sarah Lawrence College.

Lauren Magnuson is Systems and Emerging Technologies Librarian at California State University, Northridge. Her interests include PHP, Python, analytics, and data visualization, as well as promoting open-source technology in academic libraries. Magnuson has an MA in information science and an MEd in educational technology, both from the University of Missouri, as well as a BA in philosophy from Tulane University.

Dawn Paschal is assistant dean, Digital Library and ePublishing Services at Morgan Library, Colorado State University, where she led the development of a digital, institutional repository and the local electronic theses and dissertations submission program. A former catalog and area studies librarian with thirty years of professional experience, her research interests include use of primary resource materials, information seeking, and usability.

Shannon Regan is the e-journal preservation librarian with the Columbia University Libraries. Previously, she managed the electronic resource collections at Mercer University as the licensed content librarian. She has a masters of library and information science from the University of Pittsburgh.

Silvia Southwick is the digital collections metadata librarian at the University of Nevada–Las Vegas (UNLV) Libraries. Her main responsibilities include designing and maintaining a metadata application profile for UNLV digital collections; defining metadata elements and creating index guidelines for each digital collection; designing and implementing metadata quality control processes; and managing the implementation of the UNLV linked-data project. Southwick's research interests are in the areas of metadata management and linked data. She received a PhD in information transfer and a masters in library science from the Syracuse University School of Information Studies.

Laura A. Staley, the media librarian at Renton Technical College in Renton, Washington, has worked with multimedia throughout much of her career.

Teresa Yohon is a past information specialist for the Colorado Department of Education and currently conducts website usability, online content management, and online-learning studies through her company, Education and Training Connections. Current projects include development of online courses targeted to elementary teachers on the integration of financial literacy concepts into the classroom and the use of project management concepts in education.

Donald E. Zimmerman, research professor, Morgan Library Colorado State University, focuses his research on usability, website and information design, adoption of information technologies, information seeking, and environmental and health communication. Current research focuses on the usability of small-screen interfaces, adoption of e-textbooks, and faculty adoption of information technologies for teaching.